The French Colony in the Mid-Mississippi Valley

CENTER FOR FRENCH COLONIAL STUDIES
CENTRE POUR L'ETUDE DU PAYS DES ILLINOIS
WILLIAM L. POTTER PUBLICATION SERIES

THE CENTER FOR FRENCH COLONIAL STUDIES, INC.

WILLIAM L. POTTER PUBLICATION SERIES
(FORMERLY EXTENDED PUBLICATIONS SERIES)

SERIES EDITOR, BENN E. WILLIAMS

About the Center for French Colonial Studies (CFCS):

Founded in 1983, the Center for French Colonial Studies, also known as the Centre pour l'étude du pays des Illinois, promotes and encourages research into the social, political, and material history of the French colonies and French people of the Middle Mississippi Valley and the Midwest, with special focus on the Illinois Country in the seventeenth, eighteenth, and early nineteenth centuries. CFCS is organized as a 501(c)(3) corporation for exclusively charitable, literary, scientific and educational purposes. In now its third decade, the membership continues to consist of historians, archeologists, preservation technologists, architectural historians, genealogists, historic interpreters, and interested laypeople.

About CFCS's William L. Potter Publication Series:

The dissemination of knowledge forms an integral part of the organization's mission. One means to this end is the annual autumnal meeting and conference; another is the publication of the quarterly *Le Journal*, which emphasizes original research, book reviews, announcements, and news relating to the Center's mission. Recognizing a "publications gap" between shorter articles and monograph-length works, CFCS initiated its *Extended Publications Series* in order to make additional scholarship available to the public. This program publishes essays, monographs, and translations of primary documents that might not otherwise enjoy a place in print owing to their in-between length or esoteric nature. The name of the series was changed in 2011 to honor the memory of longtime series editor, board member, and past president William L. Potter.

Titles in the William L. Potter Publication Series

The Voyageur in the Illinois Country: The Fur Trade's Professional Boatmen in Mid America.
Margaret K. Brown

Jean-Baptiste Cardinal and the Affair of Gratiot's Boat: An Incident in the American Revolution
Robert C. Wiederaenders

Louis Lorimier in the American Revolution, 1777-1782: A Mémoire by an Ohio Indian Trader
and British Partisan
Paul L. Stevens

Code Noir: The Colonial Slave Laws in French Mid-America [Bilingual edition]
William Potter, editor; B. Pierre Lebeau, translator; and a preface by Carl J. Ekberg

French Colonial Studies: *Le Pays des Illinois*; Selections from *Le Journal*, 1983-2005
Margaret K. Brown and H. Randolph Williams, editors

Plumbing the Depths of the Upper Mississippi Valley. Julien Dubuque, Native Americans, and Lead Mining
With Annotated, Transcribed, and Translated Original Documents
B. Pierre Lebeau; Lucy Eldersveld Murphy; Robert C. Wiederaenders

The French Colony in the Mid-Mississippi Valley

Second edition

Margaret Kimball Brown
and
Lawrie Cena Dean

CENTER FOR FRENCH COLONIAL STUDIES
CENTRE POUR L'ETUDE DU PAYS DES ILLINOIS
WILLIAM L. POTTER PUBLICATION SERIES
NUMBER 9

The first edition of this popular work was published by American Kestrel Books, a division of American Resources Group, Ltd., under the editorship of Michael J. McNerney, who has kindly allowed the Center for French Colonial Studies to offer this revised, second edition. Thank you, our *Falco sparverius*!

THE CENTER FOR FRENCH COLONIAL STUDIES, INC.
P. O. Box 482
St. Louis, MO 63006-0482
USA

ISBN-13: 978-1479385102
ISBN-10: 1479385107

Series editor: Benn E. Williams
Front cover: Re-enactors Margaret Kimball Brown and Marv "The Colonel" Hilligoss in front of east gate at Fort de Chartres.
Back Cover: Detail of Commandant's uniform on re-enactor Marv "The Colonel" Hilligoss.
Portraits by Ken Seeber.

1. French – Illinois – History; 2. Mississippi River Valley -- History

Text composed in Garamond and Georgia

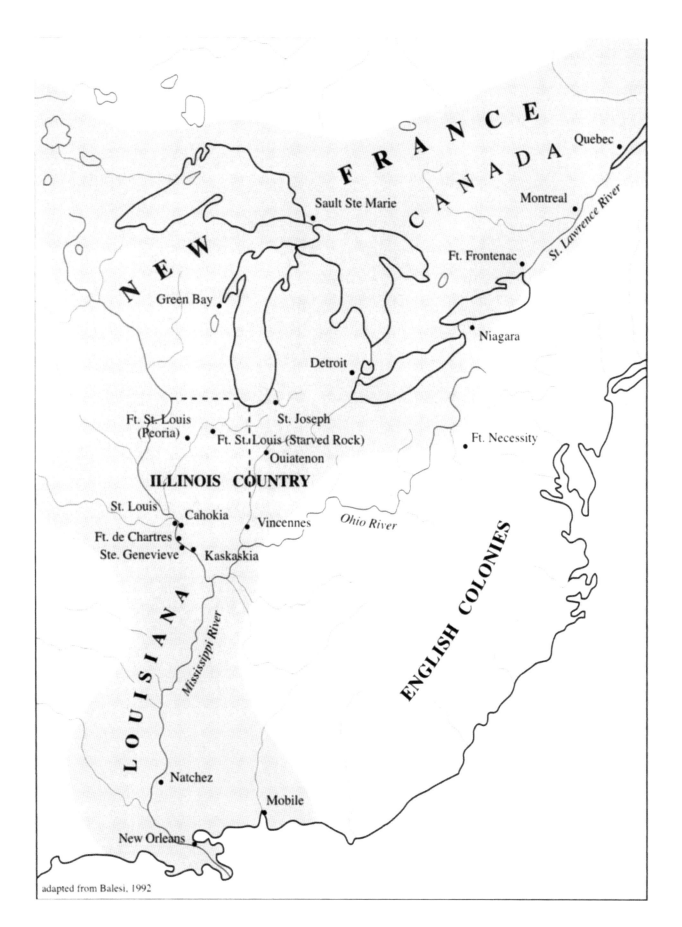

adapted from Balesi, 1992

CONTENTS

ILLUSTRATIONS

PREFACE

What were the French communities like in the eighteenth century? For a brief look, come with us on an imagined visit of the village of Kaskaskia in the 1740s. Here we find wide, dusty streets, lined with stockade-like fences, above which appear the steeply pitched roofs of houses. Opening a gate in one of these fences reveals a house of heavy upright log construction with a paneled front door and deeply-set casement windows. The path to the door is lined with flowers and herbs, in the spring the orchard at one side of the yard would be in bloom.

Inside the house are two large rooms with fireplaces and off these, smaller bedrooms. The main room, where most of the daily activities are carried out, is furnished with carved walnut chests, a vast armoire, a sideboard, tables and armchairs. Linen curtains hang at the two small windows and on the white-washed wall is a mirror.

If our imaginary visit coincided with one of the frequent balls, we might see the lady of the house dressed in her best gown of striped pink and white taffeta and red high-heeled shoes. Her husband might be wearing a green coat, vest and breeches, studded with silver buttons, all having been imported from France on the last convoy. Does this sound like the frontier? Certainly, it is not the picture received from the accounts of the later American pioneers. But French colonial life was quite different from that of the later immigrants. By the time of our imaginary visit to Kaskaskia, the French had been settled in the area for over a generation.

Where did they come from? Why did they settle here? To answer these questions we must turn back to the late seventeenth century.

ACKNOWLEDGMENTS

The authors and publisher would like to recognize the following individuals and organizations who assisted us with knowledge of the French colonial area: Ruth Gilster, Dan Malkovich, Irvin Peithmann, Ed Crow (now all deceased); Jerry and Debra Burchell, Ste. Annes Militia, Marvin "The Colonel" Hilligoss, and Dr. Charles Balesi.

EXPLORATION AND EARLY SETTLEMENT

> *On June 17, 1673, explorer Louis Jolliet and Father Jacques Marquette entered the Mississippi River, traveled its length to the Arkansas River and returned to their base at Mackinac, via the Illinois River and Lake Michigan.*

Le Pays des Illinois, the country of the Illinois, referred to the land occupied by the Illinois Indians, the Illiniwek, in the seventeenth century. By the eighteenth century, this had become a governmental designation as well. The country of the Illinois was the upper part of the French colony of Louisiana.

The Illinois Country included at least part of the present states of Illinois, Missouri, Iowa, and Indiana. The military and civil center of government was Fort de Chartres. Its jurisdiction extended from the Kansas River on the west to the Ouabache [Wabash] on the east and to the Arkansas on the south. The northern reach was not as well defined, but as the post at Peoria was garrisoned from Fort de Chartres, it apparently was included.

The Illinois Country was explored first by Canadian voyageurs; these were licensed traders looking for furs, especially for beaver, to send back to France. Not only were furs worn for warmth, but the beaver pelts were used in making felt for fashionable men's hats. Rather than catching the fur-bearing animals themselves, the voyageurs traded with the Indians, exchanging axes, knives, kettles, beads, and other items for furs. How early in the seventeenth century the voyageurs came into the Illinois Country is not known as most were illiterate and they left no record of their travels.

The trade potential attracted explorers who sought to find a waterway south to the sea; such a passage would ease the transportation problems. In 1672, Sieur Louis Jolliet formed an expedition to explore south of the Great Lakes for the waterway. Jolliet took with him five men and a Jesuit priest, Fr. Jacques Marquette.

Their travels look them across Lake Michigan through present Wisconsin and down the Mississippi River. On the journey, probably within the present state of Iowa, they encountered a village of Peoria Indians, part of the Illiniwek or Illinois nation. Jolliet and Marquette continued down the Mississippi as far as Arkansas, then, satisfied that they had found the route to the sea, began the trip back. At the juncture of the Mississippi and Illinois Rivers, they turned aside to investigate this passage back to the lakes.

On the river in northern Illinois, opposite the elevation known later as Starved Rock, they found a village of the Kaskaskia Illinois. Here, Fr. Marquette founded the mission of the Immaculate Conception, the first mission in the Illinois Country.

Figure 1: Re-enactor in typical dress of the voyageurs

Fr. Marquette returned to the infant mission for a short time in 1675, but died during his return trip to Canada. In 1678, Fr. Claude Allouez came to continue the work of the mission. By then, the village had grown and contained seven groups of the Illinois tribe, including the Peoria. Fr. Allouez counted 351 "cabins" spread out along the water's edge. Those cabins were large oval structures made from a framework of saplings bent over and fastened at the top to form a rounded roof. Woven reed mats and bark then covered the frame. These huts varied in length from 12 to 60 feet, and the larger ones might house twenty or more residents. The total population of this village is estimated to have been 5700, larger than the young French settlement of Quebec was at this time.

Figure 2: Bark lodge.

The parish that developed from the mission of the Immaculate Conception is still in existence today, over 300 years later, but it is located in southern Illinois in the heart of the old French colony on Kaskaskia Island near Chester, Illinois. How did it move down there? For that, we have to trace further the movements of the Illinois Indians.

Trade was the bond between the Illinois and the French. The lives of the Indians and the voyageurs were much alike; they both moved great distances in their activities. The traders traveled from Montreal to Illinois; the Indians went from winter camps to their summer villages along the rivers, and on war parties, slave-capturing expeditions and buffalo hunts far to the west.

Although the French government was anxious to encourage settlement in order to strengthen its claim to the central valley, the voyageurs who plied the waters of the Illinois River were not interested in colonization. Governmental wishes had little effect, but a woman's determination succeeded where officials had failed.

The woman was Marie Aranipinchicoue, the seventeen-year-old daughter of Rouensa, a Kaskaskia chief. Her father wanted her to marry a Frenchman, Michel Accault, or Ako as it is generally written. A voyageur for many years, Ako had traveled with La Salle and had accompanied Fr. Hennepin on his trip up the Mississippi and into captivity with the Sioux. Fr. Gravier, who was now in charge of the mission, said, disparagingly, that Ako was famous in the Illinois for his debaucheries.

Marie, a devout Christian, refused to marry Ako. Days of strife followed her decision. Her angry father stripped her of all her ornaments and drove her out of his cabin. Marie took shelter with other Christians while her father tried to turn the Indians against the priest whom he suspected, wrongly as it happened, of having influenced Marie's decision.

Finally, Marie decided to marry Ako with the hope of reforming him and of converting her parents to the God she worshipped. Such was Marie's character and religious fervor that she succeeded shortly in both endeavors. Ako became an upright citizen, saying to the priest that he hardly recognized himself anymore. Chief Rouensa and his fifteen-member family embraced the new religion and the majority of the Kaskaskia soon followed their chief's example and were baptized. The conversion of this large group of the Illinois greatly increased the size of the mission and gave an impetus to settlement.

Shortly after the Marie-Ako union, other French and Indian marriages took place. Jacques La Violette, who also had been with La Salle, married Catherine Ekopakineoua, Louis Delauney married Catherine Rouecanga and Antoine Baillarjon married Domitilde Choupingoua.

Figure 3: Kaskaskia India, Man Who Tracks by George Catlin.

The Illinois Indians are described as being tall and well-built, and the women must have been determined as well as attractive to get their voyageur husbands to become more settled and domestic. These Frenchmen and their wives, with the other Christian Indians, formed the nucleus from which the French colony developed.

The baptismal records for the Mission of the Immaculate Conception still exist in part and record the birth of a son, Pierre, to Marie Rouensa and Michel Ako in 1695. In the same year Catherine Delauney and Catherine La Violette also gave birth to sons. Acting as godfather on at least one occasion was Henri de Tonti (of the iron hand), La Salle's former lieutenant.

Figure 4: Holy Family Church, Cahokia, Illinois.

Few records exist for the following years. Father Gravier left the community, now located at Peoria Lakes, and did not return until 1700. When he arrived, he found that the Kaskaskia were about to leave for a proposed colony of John Law's on the Mississippi. Father Gravier hoped to stop his Kaskaskia from joining the colony and they did halt their journey south near the present site of St. Louis, Missouri on the River Des Peres. It is from this settlement that the river today still bears the name Des Peres [of the Fathers].

The French families also moved downriver to the new Kaskaskia village. In 1700, little Pierre Aka, only five years old, was sent to Quebec to receive his education. Michel Aka died, and Marie Rouensa remarried. Her new husband, Michel Philippe, had received a grant of land in Mobile and probably came upriver on a trading voyage, but he chose to remain with the Kaskaskia village rather than take his new family back to Mobile. Across the Mississippi River from Des Peres, in Illinois, was a settlement of Cahokia and Tamaroa Indians. In 1699, the mission of the Holy Family had been established at this Illinois Indian village by priests of the Seminary of the Foreign Missions. Some of the Tamaroa Indians joined the Des Peres village, and the number of French continued to increase also.

Not all the Frenchmen were in residence at one time, however, for they were busy coming and going on the river in trade. Despite the newly arrived French immigrants, the settlement on the River des Peres remained an Indian village with Indian cabins and gardens, not a colonial settlement laid out in European fashion, but this shortly was to change.

FOUNDING OF THE FRENCH COMMUNITIES

Cahokia 1699, Kaskaskia 1703, St. Philippe, Chartres, Prairie du Rocher early 1720s, Ste. Genevieve 1750s, St. Louis 1763

Fearing attacks from the Sioux Indians at the River Des Peres, on the west side of the Mississippi, the village migrated again in the spring of 1703, moving downriver to a peninsula between the Mississippi River and a tributary, the Metchigamia River, named for yet another group of Indians. This stream is now known as the Kaskaskia River from the later arrivals. Here the mission of the Immaculate Conception became a parish, and a church was built.

The village gradually acquired a larger contingent. From where did these settlers come? Initially, most of the newcomers were from Canada, but as settlers in the Gulf region became dissatisfied with conditions there, or sought new opportunities, they too moved up to the Illinois.

Although the descriptions sent back to France tend to be exaggerated, there is no doubt that the young colony was attractive compared to war-torn France, to the humid Gulf Coast, or as an escape from the long severe winters of Canada.

The ladies even venture to make this long and painful voyage from Canada, in order to end their days in a Country which the Canadians look upon as a terrestrial paradise.
This country where they are settled is one of the most beautiful in all of Louisiana and the best for the fertility of the soil. They grow wheat as fine as that in France, and all types of vegetables, root crops and herbs. There were also all kinds of fruit with very good flavor. They have in the prairies many animals such as oxen and cows.

A number of the new French immigrants married Indian women despite the government's increasing opposition to such unions. The priests approved of these marriages, maintaining

Figure 5: Sailing ship evoking the Pélican

that the women were both virtuous and industrious. There were few marriageable French women in Louisiana; most of the women in Mobile and New Orleans were already wives of colonists. To alleviate this shortage, the government proposed to ship marriageable girls from France to Louisiana.

In 1704 the vessel "Pélican" made port on the Gulf Coast in Louisiana with a cargo of girls from a convent orphanage, most of whom were promptly married. Jean Brunet *dit* Bourbonnais and his wife, Elisabeth Deshayes, a Pélican girl, soon came up to Illinois, where they would spend their long life together. But girls continued to be in short supply until those born in the New World reached marriageable age. Nicolas Michel Chassin, the royal storekeeper at Fort de Chartres, wrote back to France a complaint on his single state:

> *You see, Sir; that the only thing I now lack in order to make a strong establishment in Louisiana is a certain article of furniture that one often repents of having got and which I shall do without like the others until – the company sends us some girls who have at least some appearance of virtue. If by chance there should be some girl with whom you are acquainted who would be willing to make this journey for love of me, I should be very much obliged to her and I should certainly do my best to give her evidence of my gratitude for it.*

No girl from France volunteered, but Monsieur Chassin in 1722 married Agnes Philippe, the 16-year-old daughter of Marie Rouensa and Michel Philippe. Among the French who moved into the Illinois we find names that still exist in Illinois and Missouri today: Bienvenu, Dirousse, Duclos, Roy, Gilbert, Aubuchon, Robert, Barbeau. Many of the men had nicknames, like Jean Brunet *dit* [called] Bourbonnais. Sometimes, these names related to the area from where the man came: Blouit *dit* Le Breton, De Fosse *dit* Le Normand, and Joseph Quebado *dit* L'Espagnol [the Spaniard]. Some were probably from physical characteristics: Charle Helie *dit* Gros [big] and Jean Chabot *dit* Petit [little]; some may have been professions: Antoine Gilbert *dit* Rotisseur [roasting cook] and Henri Belmont *dit* Boulanger [baker].

The reasons for other names are obscure; they may have referred to interests, characteristic behavior, or some event in the person's life: Leonard Billeron *dit* La Fatigue [the tired one]; Antoine Pie *dit* La Plume [the feather or pen]; Francois Hennet *dit* Sanschagrin [without regret]; Louis Baudrau *dit* Va De Bon Coeur [goes with good spirit]; and Francois Cecire *dit* Bontemps [good times].

Sometimes the "*dit*" became used instead of the original surname for a branch of the family, as today La Chance and La Rose exist as surnames in Ste. Genevieve and other areas. The early settlers from whom they probably are descended were, however, named Nicolas Cailott *dit* La Chance and Andre De Guire *dit* La Rose.

Not all the Canadians in the Illinois were settled and well-behaved colonists. The voyageurs led a hard and lonely life in the wilderness and trouble was apt to result when they came to a village where wine and women were available. The priests were disturbed by this and by the bad example thus set for the Indians, and complained to the governor. In 1711, a sergeant and a group of soldiers were sent up from the Gulf coast to Kaskaskia to arrest and discipline the offenders, but the Canadians escaped into the woods. From the pen of a soldier, Penicaut, we have a brief description of the village at this time.

Penicaut was most impressed by the church which had three chapels, a baptismal font and a bell with which to summon the faithful to services. Both the French and the Kaskaskia Indians were farming the land, and oxen, cows, sheep, pigs and chickens were fairly plentiful. Flour was the important agricultural produce of the area. Wheat grew well here, which it did not do in the moist Gulf region.

Figure 6: Bread oven.

Ils ont, proche leur village, trois Moulin pour moudre leurs grains, savoir: un moulin a vent, appartenant aux RR.PP Jesuites, qui est fort employe part les habitans, et deux autres moulins a cheval, que les Illinois possedent en propre.

[translation] They have near their village three mills for grinding their grain, namely a windmill belonging to the Jesuit fathers, which is mainly used by the colonists, and two others, horsemills, which the Illinois Indians themselves own.

The voyageurs continued to create problems, and in 1718, the Company of the Indies, which had the trading concession from the Crown, posted officers and soldiers to the Illinois Country with orders to establish a fort, to bring order to the country, and to protect it from Indian attack. Pierre Dugue de Boisbriant, a cousin of Bienville, governor of Louisiana, was the commanding officer. He and his contingent of sixty-eight soldiers, *engagés* [hired workers] and convicts came up river in January of 1718 to Kaskaskia,

Figure 7: French windmill.

the population of which included both Kaskaskia and Metchigamia Indians and the French settlers.

Figure 8: Habitant.

Friction existed between the French *habitants* and the Indian community, due in part to the casual attitude of the Indians about confining their animals. The French resented the damage done by pigs in the fields and the depredations of dogs on their poultry.

The priests also decried the influence of the voyageurs on the Indian women and felt the Indians would keep the faith better at a greater distance from the French. Boisbriant attempted to solve these problems by dividing the community into three parts. The French remained at the original location, the Kaskaskia moved six miles up the Kaskaskia River, and the Metchigamia removed sixteen miles up the Mississippi to a reserve established for them (probably the first Indian reserve in the United States). Boisbriant's other mission was to construct a fort to serve as a military post for protection of the inhabitants and as the seat of military and civil government in the Illinois Country. Fort de Chartres was completed about 1720 and named in honor of the Duc de Chartres, son of the regent of France.

How was the location of Fort de Chartres selected? The reasons for Boisbriant's choice are not clear. Fort de Chartres is sixteen miles upstream from Kaskaskia, which was then the only sizable settlement in the Illinois Country. Several possible explanations for its location can be advanced. Much of the land between Kaskaskia and the fort was marshy and heavily wooded, the vicinity of the fort may have been the only place where prairie reached the bank of the Mississippi. An island existed in the river near the fort, providing shelter and a good landing for boats. The site may also have been convenient for ferrying workers to and from the lead mines which were on the Missouri side of the river around Potosi and Old Mines. However, as extant documents do not give specific reasons for the location of the fort, we are left to speculate.

ECONOMY AND TRADE

> *The voyageurs from the Illinois, for whom we were beginning to fear, have at last arrived today loaded with some flour, tallow, hams, bear grease, and furs...*

In 1711, the monopoly for trade in Louisiana was granted by the King to a Monsieur Antoine Crozat, who shortly thereafter found his expenses greater than his profits, and in 1717, the concession was transferred to John Law's Company of the West. As part of Law's attempt to revitalize the French economy, Law founded a bank and his Company of the West absorbed a number of other trading concessions to become known as the Company of the Indies.

Vast speculation in the new company occurred, eventually causing its shares to become overinflated, bringing about the collapse or the bank in 1721. The Company of the Indies survived, but hopes for the development of Louisiana were dimmed.

Figure 10: John Law

The Company of the Indies, in return for a monopoly on trade, had certain obligations to the Crown. It was to bring over colonists, increase agriculture, import slaves and search for mines. Exploring for minerals, particularly gold and silver, was an important goal; it was hoped that the lead mines would produce, not only lead, but silver as well. The mines were located on the west side of the river in present Missouri and most of the miners and slaves needed for working the mines lived there.

"Those boats are from Canada in the Batteaux form and wide in proportion to their length. Their length about 30 feet and the width 8 feet & pointed bow and stern, flat bottom and rowing six ores only ..."

--William Clark, Saturday, 20th Septr. 1806

In 1731, the Company of the Indies reported that it had built forts, supplied the garrisons for them, cleared land and even built a city (New Orleans). But having gone to this great expense, it had experienced serious reversals due in part to an uprising by the Natchez Indians in 1729. The Company requested and received permission to return the colony to the jurisdiction of the King, and so it remained until the end of the French regime in 1763.

Figure 10: "Evening Bivouac on the Missouri," Karl Bodmer, 1809-1893.

Trade in the Illinois Country was based mainly on agricultural products. The rich bottomlands were highly productive: corn [maize], wheat, and rye flourished there. Flour production was extensive. All privately owned, the mills included watermills, horsemills, and windmills for grinding flour, and bolting mills for the production of white flour. The bread consumed in the area was white bread and not, as is sometimes assumed, made from coarsely ground whole meal. Many thousands of pounds of white flour were shipped annually from the Illinois to New Orleans -- 50,000 to 100,000 pounds in a single convoy. In addition to the flour, loads of onions, hams, dried peas, salted buffalo tongues, bear oil, salt, hides, and furs were sent down river.

These goods were carried in convoys of *bateaux,* large flat-bottomed boats, constructed in Illinois. In 1746, Jean Baptiste Aubuchon, a boat builder of Kaskaskia, made an agreement with Andre Roy and Jacques Gaudefois, traders from Detroit, saying that he would construct two *bateaux.* Each *bateau* was to have a burthen of 17,000 *livres,* not including the men and supplies. [A *livre* is about the same weight as a pound; the *livre* was also a monetary unit.]

> *"It is understood that if they carry more, so much the better for the Sieurs Roy and Gaudefroy and if they carry less the said Aubuchon will make reparation to them according to the damages they suffer."*

The *bateaux* were to be delivered at the port of Kaskaskia in January complete with oars, seats, and rudders, caulked and ready to sail. Roy and Gaudefois promised to supply the nails, the iron work for the rudder, the tow and pitch for caulking. The contractor was to supply the rest.

Also used for transport were *pirogues,* hollowed out tree trunks. The *pirogues* were constructed from giant timbers and were said to be large enough to carry forty or fifty men. Official convoys from the Illinois made two round trips to New Orleans each year for trading and obtaining supplies. Private individuals also traveled the river with trade materials. The downstream trip was fairly swift, taking two to three weeks, but the return trip against the current of the river was three to four months. Public notice was given prior to the departure of the convoy, alerting anyone who might want to ship goods down river.

On fais a scavoir a tous ceux qui veuillent descendre a la mer et faire descendre leurs effets dans les bateaux du Roy de se rende lundy sixieme may au fort de Chartre pour presenter leur memoire des effets qu'ils auront a embarquer dans les dits bateau a Messieurs de La Buissoniere et La loere Flaucour...

[translation] Notice to everyone who wishes to go down to the sea and to send their goods in the boats of the King, to appear by Monday the sixth of May at Fort de Chartres to give an account of the goods which will be sent in the said boats to Mr. de la Buissoniere and De la Loere Flaucour...

Voyageurs were hired to man the boats; part of their compensation was the right to carry merchandise to be traded for their own profit. One of these contracts is given below.

On the twenty-sixth of December; one thousand seven hundred and thirty-one, before us, the notify in the Illinois, and the undersigned witness has appeared Mr. Robilliard, habitant at Fort de Chartres, who by these presents has contracted and contracts to Louis Thomas, also a habitant to descend to and return from New Orleans in his pirogue to perform during the course of the voyage everything that the said Robilliard can do for the profit and utility of the said Louis Thomas. In payment and wages for which, the said Thomas promises to give and pay to the said Robilliard the sum of two hundred livres in copper coin or in money current at the said place of New Orleans and he further promises to give passage in his pirogue for eight hams and upon the return trip for the merchandise which shall come from his wages, and to feed the said Robilliard during the course of the said voyage.

The choice of a leader for the convoy was made by the governor of the province of New Orleans as a mark of special privilege and favor. Many of the officers and soldiers who accompanied the convoy brought goods back up to the Illinois for their own profit, giving rise to frequent complaints that personal goods received preferential treatment and that military supplies destined for the Royal Storehouse were left behind on the pretext of lack of space.

> *... the person privileged begins by filled all the bateaux intended for the convoy with his goods or with those which the merchants furnish him so space is hardly to be found to load the goods of the king. To do this I was obliged to furnish a fourth bateau on the departure of the last convoy. Otherwise the King's goods would have remained here.*

Misuse of goods destined for the Royal Storehouse was also common. A certain Monsieur Tonty while in charge of a convoy one autumn, had brandy drawn from two casks which were part of the cargo. Then he ordered two men to replace the missing brandy with water.

> *They remonstrated with him to the effect that it would be better to leave the casks broached rather than to fill them with water; to which the said Sieur de Tonty replied that it would be thought that the water had been added either onboard ship or in the storehouses of the company.*

An official complained about still another convoy commander.

> *Everyone assures us that he and his detachment have been continuously drunk during the whole voyage. That will doubtless cause a generous leakage in the liquors which I had loaded on the king's account.*

Nevertheless, these convoys were vital to the survival of lower Louisiana, which was unable to produce an adequate food supply for its colonists. New Orleans was largely dependent upon supplies from France or from the Illinois Country because wheat could not be grown to maturity in its climate. An explanation of the Illinois colony's importance for New Orleans was given to the Company of the Indies in these words:

> *If war prevented you from having the sea free, this post alone could bring assistance in flam; meat and other things necessary to life to all the country that is situated on the banks of the Mississippi.*

Often, it was only the arrival of a convoy that kept famine from devastating lower Louisiana.

> *The voyageurs from the Illinois, for whom we were beginning to fear, have at least arrived today loaded with some flour, tallow, hams, bear grease, and furs...this slight assistance will not fail to give some relief to the lower part of the colony which was lacking in every provision.*

Travel up and down the Mississippi was not without peril. The river itself was dangerous; travelers speak of an overnight rise in the water level of four to eight feet. There were also the hazards of currents and of snags -- trees just below the surface of the water that might catch and overturn a boat. And the mosquitoes, everyone agreed, were the worst hazard of all.

Although most of the Indians who lived along the river were nominally friendly, during periods of warfare, such as the Natchez War in 1729, voyageurs were massacred en route. Also the Chickasaws, who were affiliated with the British and thus hostile to the French, might make forays into the region at any time.

Convoys were uncomfortable at best and deadly ill their worst. Often a person planning such a trip made his will before leaving Illinois as did the Sieur Franchomme.

In the name of the Father, the Son and the Holy Spirit, Amen. If it does not please God that I might return from the voyage I am going to undertake, I pray to Him with all my so that He may be merciful to me and grant me pardon and remission of my sins. I ask, in this case, that my wife have prayers said to God for the repose of my soul, and that she bear herself in such wise as shall render her equally estimable in the sight of God and of man...

Since I owe the Company on my own account for clothing, I shall ask my wife to sell my clothes for wheat to pay the debt. The only debt I believe I have, other than that owed by the Company is sixty livres of flour to Monsieur Basse, innkeeper in New Orleans, I beg my wife to pay it. Monsieur Laoere owes me fifty-seven livres. We owe to Pierre Bourdon and to Baillarjon each two hundred livres in beaver which is not recorded anywhere else.

Figure 11: Eighteenth-century French coins.

The Illinois Country was not only an agricultural base, but a trading depot as well. Goods shipped up from New Orleans were transferred from the Illinois base to other posts; from Fort de Chartres they went to Vincennes, Cahokia, and Peoria. Those combined military and trading posts were garrisoned from Fort de Chartres also. Kaskaskia and Fort de Chartres were both centers for trading companies and the starting points for trade up the Mississippi, Missouri, and Ohio Rivers. The company agents, after stocking up on provisions and trade goods, went out to posts among the Osage, Fox, or other Indian tribes.

It was in the winter of 1763 that the New Orleans firm of Maxent, Laclede and Company received the trading rights along the Upper Missouri. Pierre Laclede Liguest arrived at Fort de Chartres in November and wintered there, purchasing a house from Jean Girardin, a private in the troops of the Marine. Using this as his base, he searched for a good location for his trading post. An elevated site near the confluence of three great rivers, the Mississippi, Missouri, and Illinois, was selected and became the post and then the village of St. Louis.

Prices varied greatly from post to post with the cost of imported items climbing rapidly as the distance upriver increased. It was necessary always in contracts to specify the price in terms of location: flour at Illinois prices, brandy at port prices, or beaver at Ouiatenon prices, for example [Ouiatenon was near Lafayette, Indiana].

Coins were always extremely scarce, as both copper and silver coins flowed back to France to pay debts there and were hard to keep in the colony. A variety of methods was used to circumvent this problem: card money [playing cards countersigned by officers to represent a certain amount of money], bills of exchange, treasury notes, and other paper currency.

IOUs were often used in lieu of cash. If Provencal held a note indicating that Lesperance owed him 1000 *livres,* then Provencal might use this note to pay a debt to Jean Prunet. The collection of the debt then fell on Prunet's shoulders. Such notes were negotiable currency, and when one was lost or mislaid, it was necessary to cancel it in writing.

Payment in kind or by merchandise was particularly common in the early years of the colony.

Said Dutrou promises to pay to said Finet the sum of 200 livres in merchandise at the store price, payable at Christmas next.

Even houses and land were sold for merchandise when money was scarce.

I the undersigned confess to have sold, ceded and conveyed unto Antoine Francois Pelle dit *La Plume, one house with its lot and enclosures ... for the quantity of one hundred and thirty walnut boards ...*
... the quantity of two thousand livres of flour and three hundred livres of bacon for a house and lot ...

Although the colony always had within itself the resources for survival, items such as cloth, iron, guns, gunpowder, medicines, and goods to use in trade with the Indians were imported. Luxuries also came from abroad: women's high-heeled shoes, sugar, ivory billiard balls, books, coffee, and brandy. Glassware, tableware, and crockery were all imported, as were iron and brass kettles for cooking.

Figure 12: Earthenware bowl and red glazed pot belonging to Mrs. Ruth Gilster, Chester, Illinois.

Concessions of land were made to individuals by the King or his representative. Philippe Renault, a partner in the Company operating the lead mines, in addition to mining land, was given a large concession north of Fort de Chartres to grow food for his enterprise. He in turn, granted parcels of land from his concession to new arrivals, and the settlement was known as St. Philippe after his patron saint. This location was destroyed by the river in the early nineteenth century.

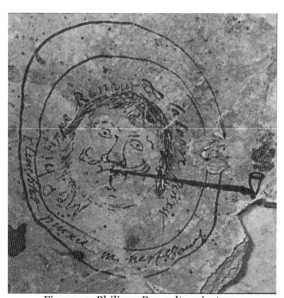

Figure 13: Philippe Renault caricature.

LAND AND VILLAGE

> *...a house for the said Lefevre twenty-one feet in length by sixteen feet in width of posts of mulberry or walnut and seven feet height to the beams.*

Very large grants also were made to several other individuals, including Lieutenant Pierre Melique, Nicolas Chassin, and Boisbriant, the commandant. These large grants were split up rapidly through further concessions being made by the grantees to new colonists. The land grants were generally one or two arpents [an arpent is about 192 linear feet] by 50 arpents in depth, extending in long, narrow strips from the Mississippi River to the bluffs at the edge of the river valley. Near the water's edge were lots where the *habitants* built their houses, farming the land further back from the river.

Although the American surveyors were to lay out the rest of the land in township squares in 1809, the long, narrow grants made over 300 years ago still show up on the modern plat maps.

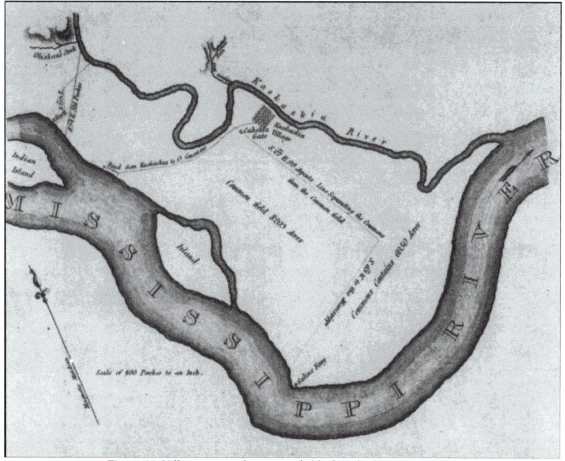

Figure 14: Village tract and common field of Kaskaskia village, 1807.

In Canada when a large tract of land was granted to an individual, he became the *seigneur* [or lord] of the *seigniory* [concession]. As part of the agreement of concession, the *seigneur* was obliged to grant most of these lands to other settlers in exchange for *cens et rentes* [tax and rent] and for three or four days of work per year for him on his lands. The *seigneur* was the only one allowed to own a flour mill, and all the inhabitants had to bring their wheat to his mill to be ground. In the Illinois Country, this system was not enforced. The land granted by the commandant or from one of the large concessions, was given in fee simple; that is, the land was owned outright with no obligations of work or rent due to anyone.

There are references to the concession of Ste. Therese Langloisiere as a *seigniory*, the area now the village of Prairie du Rocher, and to the concession of St. Philippe as the *seigniory* of Renault. However, sales of the granted lands there going from one individual to another bear such statements as the following:

> *The land is of the domain of the St. Philippe concession and has charged towards it the taxes, rent or dues, but the said vendor cannot tell the amount of these having paid nothing up to this day.* (*Source:* Brown and Dean, 1977:K214.)

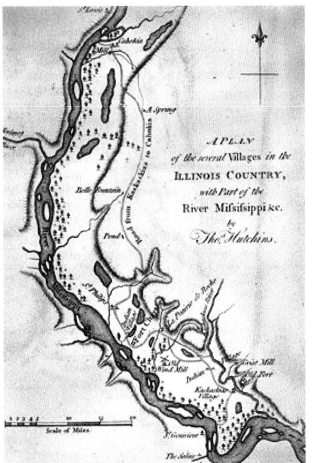

A typical individual concession reads as follows:

The Provincial Council--on the request made to us by Jacques Catherine to grant him land to settle upon, we in virtue of the powers granted to us by the Royal Indies Company have granted to the said Jacques Catherine one arpent of land by fifty in depth, running SW 1/4S, the depth NE 1/4N bounding on one side the land of Hebert the younger; on the other to the commons of Fort de Chartres ... on the condition that he shall settle there and improve the land. Failing this the said land shall be reunited to the Domain of the said Company after a year and a day, at Fort de Chartres this 2nd of May, 1724.

Figure 25: Map of the French colonial area by Thomas Hutchins, 1771

These concessions and settlements developed into small villages. There were seven French villages founded during the French regime: Cahokia, around the Indian Mission there; Kaskaskia; Prairie du Rocher; St. Philippe; the village around Fort de Chartres, which had various names; Ste. Genevieve, established some-time in the 1750s and St. Louis, developed in the mid-1760s.

In their plan, structures and organization, the villages in the Illinois reflected those of France.

> *Just as the English settlers on the seaboard brought with them their English household goods and their English institutions ... so these French of the Mississippi Valley transplanted from the heart of France their homes with their utensils and ornaments and the village community in which they and their ancestors had lived.*

The villages were the areas of concentrated settlement, but many houses were strung out along the roads that connected each settled knot with the next. Travel by land was common between settlements; roads ran from Kaskaskia to Prairie du Rocher and the Fort, on to St. Philippe and up onto the bluffs and north to Cahokia. Other roads ran from Ste. Genevieve into the mining areas. In addition to horses, light carriages are mentioned in the inventories. Carts and sledges were pulled by oxen along these roads too.

The villages were laid out in lots that were separated by the main roads and cross streets. These lots were either one arpent or 25 toises square [a linear arpent was about 192 feet and a toise was 6.39 feet]. Most houses were constructed of upright posts with *bousillage* [clay mixed with straw] filled in between the posts. The houses might be *poteaux en terre* [posts set directly into the ground], or *poteaux en solle* [posts placed on a wooden sill]. Mulberry was the most commonly used wood because of its ability to withstand dampness, but the life expectancy of a wooden house in the bottomlands was only about twenty years. Buildings were constructed also *pièce en pièce* [squared logs laid horizontally]. Stone houses and barns were constructed with limestone quarried from the nearby bluffs.

Renault built a large stone building, probably a combination residence and office, which is described in later land transactions.

> *... une maison de pierre couverte en bardeau avec quatre chiminees appellee la concession des mines situe au village de St. Philipe du Grand Marais sus parisoisse de Ste. Anile. La ditte maison composee de quatre chambres, les cloisons de planches et garnis de planches haut et bas ...*

> *[translation] A stone house with a shingled roof and four chimneys, called the concession of the mines located in the village of St. Philippe du Grand Marais [of the big swamp] in the parish of Ste. Anne. The said house has four rooms with board partitions and is floored upstairs and down.*

Figure 36: Typical French village of the 18th century. Drawing by Gordon Peckham.

The average house was about sixteen by twenty-five feet in size, and contained two main rooms, partitioned off sleeping areas, and had two doors and windows. Steeply pitched and supported by massive trusses pegged into place, the roofs were covered with thatch or, more commonly, with wooden shingles. The loft might be floored to serve as additional sleeping rooms or storage space.

Depending on the size of the house, there would be one or two fireplaces. Most chimneys were constructed of stone, but a few were made of clay laid over a framework of sticks. The latter were more apt to catch fire, although there are surprisingly few references in the records to fires. Many houses had a *galerie* or porch on two or all four sides and a small cellar for storage. The eighteenth century houses remaining in Ste. Genevieve still show many of these architectural details.

A contract describes the details of construction for one house:

> *... a house for the said Lefevre twenty-one feet in length by sixteen feet in width of posts of mulberry or walnut and seven feet high to the beams ... double beams of four and a half inches thick by eight wide; one door on one of the long walls and two windows; the door to be two feet two inches wide and five feet four inches high; the windows two feet wide and three and a half high ... the said house to be plastered ...*

In 1723, the storehouse of the Company of the Indies, located in the first Fort de Chartres, had a central hallway walled with whitewashed, tongue-and-groove boards and two offices on each side. The exterior had folding doors, and there were shuttered casement windows. In 1727, a new Commandant's residence was built; measuring fifty-five by thirty feet, it had a central hallway with a store room at the back. On each side of the hall was an apartment with two rooms and a kitchen. Each apartment contained a walnut cupboard with double doors, walnut side board, dresser, kneading trough, tables with folding leaves and chairs.

The interior walls of houses were whitewashed and sometimes paneled and plastered. The furnishings might include dropleaf tables, chairs, armchairs, chests, sideboards, cupboards, etc.

A bedstead with curtains was an important piece of furniture. The marriage contract often specified its ownership in the event of the death of one of the couple. Furniture was made of walnut, so plentiful locally that even pig troughs are noted as being of walnut!

Private dwellings also served other functions; they were used as shops, boarding houses, or inns and many had billiard rooms. Billiards apparently was a very popular entertainment. An extra room attached to the main building would house the billiard table and equipment. An inventory of a billiard lists both large and small balls; the game was quite different from that played today. An ivory billiard ball was found in archaeo-logical work at Kaskaskia.

The lots were fenced with posts and within the fence beside the house was a garden, which provided most of the family's vegetables. The lot also might contain a well, pigeon house, stable and hen house. On the lot would be the bread oven too, a domed structure about six feet long and three feet wide, made of puddled clay laid over a wooden framework and fired to a cement-like hardness. Large barns were built on the village lot or on nearby farming strips; sixty by forty feet was a common size for a barn.

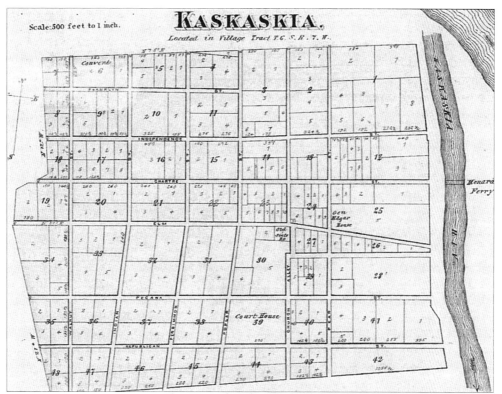

Figure 47: Plat of Kaskaskia, 1875.

Figure 18: Early Ste. Genevieve mural at Missouri Capitol in Jefferson City, Missouri.

Each village had its own church. The parish of the Immaculate Conception was at Kaskaskia, of course; the parish of Ste. Anne was at the village of Fort de Chartres with chapels at Prairie du Rocher [St. Joseph's] and St. Philippe [the Visitation]. Holy Family mission remained at Cahokia and St. Joachim's was at Ste. Genevieve. The first church in St. Louis, dedicated to St. Louis, was constructed in 1770.

Specifications exist for a proposed stone church to be constructed at Kaskaskia in 1740. The church was to be seventy-two feet long by forty-six feet wide with a semicircular apse twenty-six feet in diameter. The church was to be lighted by ten windows in each long wall and to have a main door fifteen feet high and eight feet broad. The church of Ste. Anne at the Fort de Chartres village was a simple frame construction, post on sill, fifty by thirty feet in size with walls eleven feet high. The churches each elected churchwardens to regulate the affairs of the vestry and certain aspects of the community's social life.

POPULATION AND GOVERNMENT

The colony never grew very large; a census taken in 1723 by Diron D'Artagette, the Inspector General, gives the total number of persons at Fort de Chartres, Kaskaskia, and Cahokia as 334. This figure does not include the garrison at Fort de Chartres, numbering around seventy persons at the time, but only the *habitants* and resident traders. In 1732, Fort de Chartres, Kaskaskia, and St. Philippe are listed as having 388 inhabitants, and by 1752, the population had risen to about 2000. These figures again omit the garrison, which generally numbered between 200 and 300 men in the later period.

In their Royal Charter, the Company of the Indies was directed to encourage immigration in order to increase the productivity of Louisiana, but the yearly quota of immigrants set in the charter was never met. Why was this rich and productive area so underpopulated? The French government had little interest in colonization as a goal in itself. Due to the long series of wars in Europe, France was depopulated and needed her citizens at home for farming and for the armies. Louisiana was viewed as a potential source of wealth for the homeland, as Mexico was to Spain, an alluring prospect to a government impoverished by wars, extravagance, and inflation. But when gold and silver were not found in Louisiana, official interest in the province faded.

However, the colony's strategic importance in preventing British or Spanish encroachment into the interior of the continent, and the contributions of its agricultural production were recognized.

> *If only the strength and solidity of settlements are considered, the decision should be to people Louisiana on the upper river. It should draw its chief strength and its principal resources from the Post of the Illinois ... [which] seems placed where it can always, despite all the navies in the world, export grain and meat.*

The Illinois Country was potentially a major power center for the French, available for building a French empire in North America that could dominate the entire upper Mississippi River and Great Lakes regions. Had this potential been realized, the relative strengths of France and Britain in the New World would have been greatly altered.

The Illinois colony did possess a status different from other posts in Louisiana, not only because of its ideal position to control the important central valley, but also because it was one of the few settlements that remained consistently inhabited and stable throughout the French regime. Its unique position was recognized in 1722 by the formation of a Provincial Council to govern the Illinois Country. In 1716, the King had established a Superior Council in New Orleans as the governmental body regulating all military and civil matters in Louisiana.

The first Provincial Council of the Illinois consisted of four members: Boisbriant as first lieutenant of the King, commanding in the Illinois and serving as Judge; Marc Antoine de la Loire des Ursins, principal clerk of the Company of the Indies and first councilor; Nicolas Michel Chassin (remember him?), Keeper of the Royal Storehouse and second councilor; Andre Perillau as clerk for the Council and secretary of the Council. Additional members were appointed to the Council to hear criminal cases.

The cases that came before the Provincial Council were varied and the few that survive contain interesting vignettes of the life in the colony. A certain Claude Chetivau appeared before the Council twice, once for attempted desertion, at which time the following description of his background and appearance is given:

Figure 19: French playing cards.

... we went to the prisons of Fort de Chartres where we found a man about five feet four inches tall with curly gray hair, gray beard, gray eyes and an aquiline nose .... We have asked him his name, that of his father and mother; the place of his birth, his age, his trade and his religion. He replied his name was Claude Chetivau, son of Nicolas Chetivau and Antoinette Lagruy, native of Soissons, diocese of the said place, fifty-five years of age, cook by trade and of the Catholic, Apostolic and Roman faith.

He was found guilty of attempting to desert. His sentence? He was ordered to stay! He did so and promptly got into more difficulties; he was accused of cheating at cards. Jacques Brochard claimed that the deck of cards used in a game won by Chetivau was marked, and he accused Chetivau of defrauding him of 600 livres and wanted restitution and damages. Chetivau's defense was that Brochard marked the cards after the game was done, and the debt was paid.

Thus it was a frivolous pretext on the part of the said Brochard in order to gain restitution of his loss, to allege after the fact that the deck of cards, which he has in his possession and could easily have falsified or cut however he wished, was indeed falsified or cut by said Chetivau, which the said Chetivau formally denies. And if such reasoning is allowed, the said Brochard would have an unfair advantage; that is, when he wins as he often does, he may keep silent and when he loses, he will not have to pay.

The final disposition of the case is not given. Chetivau brought several witnesses in his favor, and he may have won his case.

Guillaume Liberge witnessed and later testified in court about a fight at the house of Daniel Richard in Kaskaskia. Taunts were exchanged between Richard and a man named Catin; they cursed and ripped each other's shirts. Still fighting, they tumbled into another room where another Richard, nicknamed the Parisian, was sitting. Liberge said he tried to calm the dispute by offering a shirt to replace Catin's torn garment. Snubbed by the combatants, Liberge retired to the kitchen to smoke his pipe in peace. Shortly thereafter, he heard both men shouting they were being murdered. He paused to get a candle, and upon trying to enter the room found Richard the Parisian with an axe in his hand, blocking the door and threatening to break his head if he came any further. However, Liberge did eventually succeed in separating Catin and Daniel Richard who were still grappling with each other. The two Richards left and Liberge tended to Catin who was wounded in the back by an axe blow.

Both Richards were put on trial for the dis-turbance, and each accused the other of striking the blow from which Catin eventually died. Before his death, Catin told the surgeon, Rene Roy, and also the Royal Attorney, Joseph Buchet, that Daniel Richard was the one who struck him. After many witnesses were interviewed, the case was finally settled. Both Richards were fined 100 *sous*, to be given to the poor of the parish.

Soldier   Soldier   Soldier

(summer dress)   *(western outposts)*

Sergeant

Cadet "a l'Eguillette"   *Officer*   *Drummer*

Figure 20: French Colonial Infantry (Compagnies Franches de la Marine) in North America and the West Indies, circa 1740-1763.

Figure 21: Brandy bottle.

LIFE IN THE COMMUNITY

...a woman's outfit of striped satin lined with taffeta, rose colored, with one pair of silk hose, shoes, socks, and mitts...

The French villages in the Illinois had ways to meet other social and legal needs that were not served by the Provincial Council or the church. Among the other officials was a *huissier* [bailiff], one at Kaskaskia and one at Fort de Chartres, whose duties were to serve summons, bring in miscreants, and to read *"in a loud and audible voice"* at the church door after Mass any important decrees or announcements of public auctions. Another official, called a syndic, was elected to enforce the ordinances concerning the commons and other decisions made by the occasional assemblies of the settlers.

Figure 22: Re-enactor portraying a French blacksmith.

The commons and common fields attached to each village were used by all settlers for grazing their cattle and horses. Ordinances were passed giving the date when cattle were to be allowed into the common fields to graze and when they had to be removed to allow for planting. Each land owner whose property adjoined the commons was responsible for maintaining his section of fence, and this needed frequent enforcement.

An important figure in the busy, litigious life of the settlers was the notary. He was called on to write marriage contracts, wills, estate inventories, and settlements, acknowledgments of debt, payments of debt, sales of real estate, sales of slaves, contracts for business and trade, building contracts and specifications, and numerous other documents. The notary was often clerk of court also and kept transcripts of the proceedings, taking depositions and recording the testimony of witnesses and the decisions rendered by the court. It was a full-time profession combining elements of present-day lawyer, county clerk, court stenographer and notary public. The notary collected fees for his work and kept a copy in his files of each document he executed. These files, later turned over to the British, have given us most of our knowledge of life in French Illinois and are the source of many of the quotations in this book.

No government official was directly responsible for social welfare, that is, to see to the needs of the indigent, the elderly, orphans, or widows. However, this was managed through other legal mechanisms within the community. Children were placed in the care of an administrator and guardian, who was responsible for managing the minors' property until they were of age. Legal majority was not attained until twenty-five years of age, except through a special emancipation petition.

Widows generally remarried quickly and the new husband would agree in the marriage contract to take responsibility for the children of the previous marriage.

The relationship as a baptismal godparent held a responsibility for orphaned children. Jean Baptiste Becquet and his wife agreed to take the orphaned Pierre Texier, Becquet's godson, to live with them to teach him Becquet's trade of locksmithing.

Many of the elderly, when they found the burden of farming too much for them, arranged to make a donation of their goods and lands to a relative or friend, who would in exchange agree to care for them until their deaths, In 1751, Jean Brunet *dit* Bourbonnais and his wife Elisabeth made a gift of their house, lot and goods to Pierre Aubuchon, their daughter Elisabeth's husband. They also forgave the rest of the debt owed them by Aubuchon for a house he had purchased from them, Aubuchon promised to care for them and maintain them for the remainder of their lives.

In 1742, Antoine Ple *dit* La Plume, another early settler, donated to Louis de La Margue de Marin and his wife, all his property, consisting of a house, slave, livestock and furniture upon the condition that they maintain him for the rest of his life, give him *100 livres* a year spending money and at his death, pay his funeral expenses.

What care and maintenance involved is detailed more fully in another such donation. Nicolas Boyer and his wife Dorothee Olivier agreed to care for her parents, Jean and Marthe Olivier, for the rest of their lives in return for donation of all their property. The Oliviers will be given:

A house or a room appropriate for the lodging of two venerable persons, well-heated, snug and sheltered from rain and bad weather: if they are obliged to have their meals and housekeeping separately, they will be allowed to keep all the furniture, pots, pans, and kettles included in the donation. They will be furnished for each year with:

1500 livres of good, sound, true, and merchantable flour (for whose storage they are responsible)
30 cords of fire wood
5 fat pigs
4 cartloads of maize
2 minots [a dry measure] of salt
1/2 livre of pepper
2 minots of peas
1 minot of beans
30 pots of bear oil
30 livres of suet

1/2 livre of candle wick
25 livres of good smoking tobacco

Figure 23: Re-enactors portraying French women in garden.

The sum of 200 livres to buy clothing and linens for their personal use during the course of the year, coverings for their bed, which consist in this country of tanned buffalo robes, to be replaced as necessary.

The grantees promise to have their clothing and linen washed and cleaned as necessary and to furnish generally all they will need both in health and in sickness, medicines, surgeon's visits, meat and poultry for broths and consommés, and people to nurse them and after the death of each of them, to have them interred.

Illegitimate children, by order to the Provincial Council, were supported by the father, as indicated by one case:

To Monsieur the judge in the Illinois, Jacques Bernard dit *St. Jacques humbly petitions you saying that his wife has had a child with one Pierre Hulin during his absence at the port, which causes him great distress. He has resource to you,*

Monsieur; to beg you most humbly to do him justice in this event and that it may please you to order the said Pierre Hullin to take charge of his child ... and that the said Pierre Hullin be condemned to pay for the feeding of the child from his birth to the present. With the scandal he has created which reflects both on the church and the said St. Jacques, and that the said Pierre Hullin may be condemned to pay all expenses, damages and interest.

Figure 24: Re-enactors portraying French carpenters with 18th-century tools.

There was no unemployment problem however, for there was always enough work to go around. Agricultural workers were needed to work the farm land and to clear and prepare new land for production. Trade demanded strong, tireless men to paddle the boats and to haul heavy packs across portages. Agriculture and trade were the major occupations of the villagers and every *habitant* had a large garden to produce food for the table and for winter needs.

Other more specialized trades and occupations were present such as roofer, carpenter, cabinet maker, gunsmith, blacksmith, tailor, innkeeper, baker, laundress, shop keeper, cooper, cartwright, sawyer, mason, boat builder, vintner, and brewer. There was even a schoolmaster, one Francois Cottin, who paid Pierre Aubuchon for an arpent of land by contracting for two years to teach one of his children to read and write. In the deed, Cottin agrees to *"push the child as far as she is able to learn, to give him two lessons a day according to the custom of masters of this art, with assiduity and vigilance ..."* The use of both the feminine and masculine pronouns in the document leaves it uncertain whether the child was a girl or boy.

Books are mentioned in a few household inventories and some inhabitants were educated as demonstrated by their handwriting or signatures. Others laboriously wrote or printed their names and probably could write

Figure 25: Re-enactor at 18th-century lathe.

little else. Many could not write at all and made an "X" on their contracts. Some of the women, however, were able to sign their names, so whatever education was available was not confined entirely to males.

One important profession was that of the doctor. Surgeons were attached to the garrison at the Fort. They also cared for the civilian population and acted as coroner when necessary. They possessed the best medical knowledge and medicines of the time and probably also were familiar with Indian herbal medicines. In 1739, the King's merchant fleet was supplied with the following medicines for New Orleans:

Brandy
Balm of Fern
Epsom salts
Senna
Gooseberry syrup
Laudanum
Dragon's blood
Salpetre
Oil of sweet almonds
Camphor
Syrup of lemon
Ammonia salt
Syrup of licorice
Rattlesnake oil
Blistering ointment
Castororeum
Ipecac-quinine
Oil of vitriol
Turpentine
Rhubarb
Essence of Juniper berry
Extract of Hyacinth
Flower of camomile
Syrup of plain chicory

In 1739, a large building in the village of Chartres was purchased from Cesar De Blanc by the King for a hospital, and a contract was made with Renee Drouin to launder the patients' linen, the sheets, shirts and bandages. Rene Roy, the surgeon, supplemented his income by contracting to supply foodstuffs to the hospital, eggs, milk, fresh meat (when available) and vegetables.

In addition to the colonists with their various trades, professions and occupations, there was another group of workers, the black and Indian slaves. The Indian slaves were generally from western tribes and had been acquired by the Illinois Indians on war parties. The black slaves came from Africa, or from the West Indies, to New Orleans and up river. Some slaves were employed in Renault's mining activities but most worked on the farms or as oarsmen on convoys.

The *Code Noir* (the legal code governing black slaves in Louisiana) directed that slaves should be baptized and married in the church and that slave families should not be broken up by sales. Prominent and influential members of the community, including the commandant, appear in the baptismal records as godparents to black slaves. Separate houses were provided for the slave families, and generally they seemed to have been treated well, even if only for economic reasons, for the value of a slave was double that of a house and land. Many of the garrison's soldiers deserted into the woods, but few of the black slaves went, although they were welcomed by the Indians if they did flee.

Records exist of emancipations, the most common form being an agreement by an owner that upon his death his slave would be freed, but emancipations during the lifetime of the owner also occurred. According to the *Code Noir,* a freed black had the same rights and privileges as free-born persons. They were full citizens, had the right to own property, make contracts, serve in the militia and otherwise participate in the community. Andre, a free black at Fort de Chartres made an *engagement* [contract] with Melique to serve as a domestic for a year.

Duverger, a black voyageur originally from New Orleans, purchased a house in Kaskaskia in 1739 for 800 livres, which he paid in full by October of 1740. In another contract, he hired a Frenchman for the winter hunt and to go to New Orleans to sell the meat. He appears to have had some medical training, for he is referred to as a surgeon and received payment from a Frenchman for medical treatment. Duverger died in 1743. He was married and when he died, his wife was still a minor so a guardian was appointed for her and the estate, the standard procedure.

Under the French regime, both blacks and women enjoyed rights that they were not to have again for well over a century and a half. The position of women in eighteenth century Illinois depended, however, on their marital status. In the contract of marriage made prior to the religious ceremony, certain rights of the woman to property or money in the event of the death of her spouse were specified. A married couple held property jointly, but a wife could not sell land without her husband's permission. If, however, the land in question was part of her inheritance, her agreement was necessary for the sale. Widows and women separated from their husbands had the right to buy and sell property. Some women appear in the records hiring voyageurs, and they could carry on trade.

Women were known throughout their lives by their maiden name; Madame Hervy appears in the documents as Renee Drouin; however, after her husband's death she might also be called the Widow Hervy. The French women were more "liberated" than were their English counterparts on the east coast, or the American women who came later into the prairies.

Indeed, many of the images of pioneer life based on the later westward expansion are not applicable to the French colony Illinois. Log cabins, sod huts, dirt floors, and oiled skin windows were not for the French. Nor did they like to wear dull brown and gray homespuns. In addition to more utilitarian materials, fine fabrics were imported; bright colors were favored by all.

A fine lady's gown, perhaps the latest Paris fashion, is described in a sale:

... a woman's outfit of striped satin lined with taffeta, rose colored, with one pair of silk hose, shoes, socks and mitts ...

A trader-farmer had in his possession:

... two pairs of silk hose, 2 pairs of wool hose, 2 silk handkerchiefs, 22 shirts, 2 pairs cotton breeches, cotton vest, 2 red caps, 1 pair woman's shoes, sergeant's uniform of munitions cloth.

Fine garments were not worn all the time of course, and more coarsely woven woolen goods, hides and furs were common, but dress was important to everyone, as evidenced by the following description of the wages to be paid to one voyageur:

A complete suit of camleteen [woolen cloth woven with mohair or silk] with silk lining, to wit: a green coat and 2 pairs of breeches, one fine half beaver hat, 4 good and fine shirts trimmed with good cambric, a pair of silk hose of a color suitable to the rest.

The furnishings used in the homes were made in the colony, but the pieces were not crude for they were built by master cabinet makers who had emigrated from France. Many smaller items were imported directly from France, including some very fine and costly luxuries such as mirrors, silver goblets, diamond buckles, crystal salt cellars, a horn and silver snuff box, a watch, a sundial, books, tapestries, carpets and twelve prints of ancient emperors (hung in a billiard hall).

The quantity and quality of the goods, as might be expected, varied with the economic standing of the person. Inventories made at the death of an individual offer detailed information on the kinds, amounts and quality of personal possessions. In 1724, Legras, a hunter assigned to the convoy of Monsieur Demoy, died while on the voyage. Some of his goods were inventoried and sold; although he had few possessions he appears to have been careful of his appearance.

case with two razors
great coat of limbourg
a comb
a pair of silk hose
half a bar of soap
a pair of woolen hose
pocket knife
5 linen shirts
1 qt. brandy

2 gun worms
2 trade guns
an old casket without a key
a broken gun
2 pairs of Indian moccasins
an old blanket of dog hair

A more prosperous trader, the same Antoine de Tonty mentioned earlier as leader of a convoy, died in 1737, and his goods were inventoried:

> *A house of post in the ground construction, 20 x 15 feet with a straw roof; 2 cows; 5 carrots of tobacco; 2 old broken guns; 2 candlesticks; snuffers and tray of copper; 1 mattress; one small pillow; a pair of old sheets.*

> *Used half beaver hat trimmed with silver; five suits, one with a vest of coffee colored broadcloth; another vest of gray woolen broadcloth; vest and breeches of camleteen; two pairs of breeches in poor condition; 8 used shirts; pair used silk hose; 2 aunes [measure of cloth] of batiste.*

> *A coffer with a key; one broken case with 10 flasks, five are broken; small casket; spade; a pair of andirons; spit; two poor pewter salt cellars; 18 pewter plates and 2 platters; 1 yellow copper basin; one old skimmer.*

Jean Baptiste Baron both traded and farmed, as did most men; he was a solid middle-class citizen. From the previous descriptions of the agricultural richness of Illinois Country, it is obvious that a hard working farmer-trader might amass a good deal of property. The following inventory was made on the death of Marie Catherine, J. B. Baron's wife. Many of the terms used for the fabrics are not translated because it is difficult to find present day equivalents for them:

Figure 26: Period rifle.

> *Three frock coats of calmande and monchiton, lined with carise*
> *1 hooded greatcoat, vest and breeches, unlined, of morocco*
> *1 hooded greatcoat of Cadiz and 1 black vest*
> *2 vests of cholet and 1 hooded greatcoat of blue limbroug*
> *1 hooded greatcoat with false silver braid and 1 vest of camlet also with silver braid, silver buttons*
> *1 hair purse and 1 half beaver hat*
> *1 wool belt and 1 pair of gloves*
> *1 pair of silk stockings and 1 of wool*

3 breeches, 1 large of cotton, 1 of bombazine and the other of Cadiz
5 shirts of laval
2 shirts of Beaufort
1 dressing gown and petticoat of taffeta, one cotton gown, one same of India cloth and its petticoat
1 pair of men's silver buckles
I malacca cane with a tombac handle, 1 hunting knife, one cavalryman's pistol, 2 old pairs of shoes
3 taffeta purses, 1 pair of men's wool stockings and 1 pair of child's wool stockings
4 women's gowns
8 petticoats and skirts
8 short capes
3 black coifs, 2 crimson coifs, 6 fichus, 1 pinafore
1 pair of embroidered shoes
1 valise
4 old pairs of women's silk hose
5 women's blouses

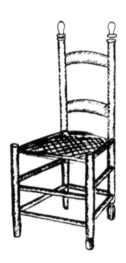

Figure 27: Period chair.

In their living quarters, the Barons had curtains at the windows and a carpet on the floor, as well as having valuable items such as mirrors.

3 window curtains of brown cloth and 3 of India cloth
1 carpet of India cloth
2 chests with locks
2 caskets with locks, covered with red copper
1 large mirror with a curved frame
1 armchair and 7 old chairs, all plain and without decoration
1 square table, turned, with 1 drawer
2 covered caskets gilded red copper
1 yellow copper candlestick

1 small mirror with frame
20 napkins, both plain and worked
5 tablecloths, one worked, 3 of Beaufort and the other of Hautbrin.

Figure 28: Drop-leaf wooden table.

Their kitchen was well equipped, both with necessary items, such as two pot hooks with chains to suspend the covered kettles over the cooking fire, and more luxurious items, such as three silver goblets and two crystal goblets and:

3 bottle cases, one with 6 bottles, one with 9
1 small tin ladle
1 pewter funnel
26 plates, 2 large platters, 1 small, 1 pot, 1 pewter salt cellar; 32 iron forks, 10 spoons and a small pewter basin
6 earthenware plates, glazed in white
1 dish cupboard with its buffet
1 old round baking dish and 1 small cauldron used as a drinking cup
2 frying pans, 1 grill and 1 fork for taking meat out of the pot
4 medium pots, one of which has a broken foot
1 minot of salt
1 medium cauldron, 1 small copper kettle and 1 pail

Figure 35: Hand-blown blue-green bottles.

The bedrooms were furnished with three feather beds, a bedstead with a feather bed, three small beds and two straw mattresses. There were two bolsters, three pillows, five sheets, a green wool blanket, a blue wool blanket and a green wool counterpane.

Baron had farm land, house lots, cattle and slaves, all of which are in his inventory.

1 lot of land where the said Baron lives, upon which is built a house with a stone basement, gardens, a courtyard and other lodgings and commodities
1 piece of land 3 arpents wide running from the Rigolet to the hills
1 house, lot 3 arpents wide, 1 barn
1 female Indian slave, 8-9 years old
1 family of slaves consisting of 1 male negro, 1 epileptic female Indian and a female child at the breast
1 male Indian slave about 8 years old
5 medium pigs and 4 newborn ones
9 oxen, 6 broken and 3 others running in the woods
6 cows, 3 with a calf
9 heifers and 1 bull running in the woods
2 work horses
2 mares, 1 last year's filly, 1 this year's colt
40 poultry, large and small

The list of Baron's tools and goods illustrates his dual role as farmer and trader and includes both farm implements and trade goods.

80 minots of wheat
1 old horse harness
1 scythe forge, 2 old scythes, 4 new scythes
3 varnished yokes
4 axes and two augers
1 new plow apparatus
1 old hay cart and 1 tip cart without wheels
1 iron mold for lead
7 sickles, 2 long saws
42 packets of tanned buckskins, 400 livres of lead
300 livres of tallow
28 trade axes, 19 tomahawks
38 trade pickaxes
10 packets of beaver
2 packets of bobcat

There is a surprising omission from these lists—guns. Only two broken ones and a cavalry pistol are mentioned here. It does not appear, from the inventories at least, that the average householder lived with his musket ready to hand.

THE MILITARY AND THE FORT

Construction Date:
Fort de Chartres I, 1720-21
Fort de Chartres II, 1725-26
Fort de Chartres III, 1755

Figure 30: Fort de Chartres.

All able-bodied *habitants* were in the local militia. A militia company was organized for each village, the first being commissioned in 1723 at Kaskaskia by Diron D'Artaguette, the Inspector General.

> *I called together all the inhabitants of this village to whom I said I had an order from the King to form a company of militia for the purpose of putting them in a position to defend themselves ... so I formed a company, after having selected four of the most worthy among them to put at the head. This company being under arms, I passed it in review the same day.*

The militia captain was required to muster the men periodically and to be sure they had at least some military training and discipline. The militia was not merely a defensive organization; its members could be called out to accompany the regular soldiers from Fort de Chartres. In fact, the militia received similar training to the soldiers.

> *M. de Macarty will give special attention to the bourgeois militia companies, making them assemble frequently in each place to drill, and having them learn the drill recently ordered by His Majesty of which we have sent several copies both for the militia of each place and for the troops whom he will take care to have well disciplined.*

Although no battles were ever fought at Fort de Chartres, the militia and the soldiers were involved in campaigns against the Indians from the Fox Wars in 1728 to the French and Indian War in the late 1750s. In 1729, the Natchez Indians on the lower Mississippi rose against the French and massacred 235 settlers near their village. Soldiers from Fort de Chartres were engaged in the punitive action taken by the French against the Natchez.

The Chickasaw, who were under British influence, frequently attacked French convoys and a series of engagements were carried out against them. The most disastrous battle for the Illinois French was in 1736 when a force from Fort de Chartres, consisting of militia and regular soldiers was annihilated by the Chickasaws. The commandant, many officers, soldiers and militia were killed, resulting in a grievous loss for the Illinois community.

The soldiers of the military post of Fort de Chartres were colonial troops organized in independent companies recruited by their captain and under the regulation of the *Ministère de la Marine* (Ministry of the Navy). A company was supposed to consist of: 1 captain, 1 lieutenant, 1 ensign, 1 cadet *"a l'éguillette"* [son of an officer or gentleman who was being trained as an officer], 1 soldier cadet, 2 sergeants, 3 corporals, 2 drummers and 41 soldiers.

A Swedish visitor to Canada in the 1750s described the soldier's life as follows:

The soldiery enjoy such advantages here as they are not allowed in any part of the world... They get every day a pound and a half of wheat bread ... They likewise get plenty of peas, bacon, and salt or dried meat .... All the officers kept cows .... The soldiers had each a small garden outside the fort, which they were allowed to attend and to plant in it whatever they liked... and planted all kinds of vegetables. In time of peace the soldiers have very little guard duty .... Each soldier got a new coat every two years; but annually, a waistcoat, cap, hat, breeches, cravat, two pair of stockings, two pair of shoes, and as much wood as he had occasion for in the winter. They likewise got five sols apiece every day, which is augmented to thirty sols when they have particular labor for the King.

Although these provisions seem generous, in practice things did not always work out so well. Pay was slow in coming, coinage was always scarce and uniforms were not sent regularly or were of very poor quality. However, there was no shortage of food stuffs in Illinois and during their service, many soldiers rented or purchased houses with gardens. Generally, two or three soldiers formed a partnership, enabling one to stand guard duty or to go with the convoy while the others took care of the house and garden. Some soldiers, when their tour of duty was up, elected to remain in Illinois and were given grants of land.

The number of soldiers actually housed within Fort de Chartres may not have been very large and apparently consisted of those on guard duty and soldiers who did not have the funds, or perhaps the interest, in acquiring a house and land. Although residences were supplied for the commandant and the royal storekeeper, they also maintained homes in either Kaskaskia or the village of Chartres.

The description of the first fort, the one that Boisbriant built in 1720-21 is very brief; it was square with two bastions but neither the dimensions nor details of the interior structures are given. In a report in 1725, Bienville the governor of Louisiana, wrote: *"The post of the Illinois is very old and there has never been any fort there except the one that M. Boisbriant built in 1721."* In March of 1725, plans were underway for construction of a new fort. A contract was concluded with eight soldiers of the garrison who agreed to dig a trench three feet deep and to place posts in it. The contract says to *"double the fort with stakes"* which would appear to mean a double wall of posts. The soldiers also were instructed to remove any tree stumps found in the way and to construct loopholes every five feet. Also, a contract was let to Lieutenant Melique in November of 1725 to provide materials for construction of a powder magazine.

Figure 31: Bienville, Governor of Louisiana.

The second fort, constructed in 1725-26, was still standing in 1732 when it was described in the inventory taken at the retrocession of the colony by the Company of the Indies to the Crown. The fort was small, 25 *toises* on a side [about 160 feet], with four projecting bastions. On the interior were four buildings: the residence of the commandant and storekeeper, a guard house, barracks with a gunsmith's forge and another house. Each bastion contained a structure: the powder magazine, a prison with a pigeon house above it, a chicken house, and a stable. It was in severe disrepair.

Another, third fort appears to have been constructed out on the prairie away from the river and the flooding. Apparently this one was refurbished and maintained until 1747, when its ruinous condition forced the transfer of most of the garrison to temporary quarters at Kaskaskia. An early aerial photograph revealed a dark soil stain outlining a square fort with four bastions, probably this fort. Archaeological testing was done in that location in 1983-84, and two walls of this fort were located, the north and south, spaced one *arpent* apart. A single row of upright posts for the palisade had been placed in a trench about three and a half feet deep. The posts had been pulled out when the location was abandoned.

By 1747, it was obvious that a new fort was necessary, and the availability of local stone made it a good choice for the construction material for a new fort. Vaudreuil, the governor of Louisiana at the time, was not only interested in new construction, but also in a new location for the fort. He commented that *"the village of L'Establissement [the village around Fort de Chartres] up to the present has been the principal post, without the reason for it being well understood."* Vaudreuil was determined to place the fort at

Colonial Engineer
c. 1750-1760

Army Engineer
c.1750-1755

Army Engineer
1758-1763

Army Engineer
1756-1758

Figure 32: French engineers, New France, 1750-1763.

Kaskaskia, which was the major mercantile settlement, and in 1751, he ordered Macarty, the new commandant to make his residence at Kaskaskia. This order was repeated in his instructions to Francois Saucier, the royal engineer, who was also to prepare cost estimates for both wooden and masonry forts. The design of the fort, Vaudreuil directed, was to be a square with four bastions, with a rampart about ten feet wide supported by an interior wall which could also serve as a wall of the buildings. The fort was to be large enough to hold 300 men and a year's rations.

In January of 1752, Macarty reported large quantities of stone and lime for mortar had been ordered. In March, he reported that Saucier's plans for the new fort were nearly finished, commenting that "this fort is well located for the present," an apparent reference to the site of the other fort. In his reply, Vaudreuil insisted again that a fort near Prairie du Rocher was too far from Kaskaskia. No letter has been found with an agreement to build the new fort 60 toises [383 feet] from the previous fort as is noted on Bellin's map of the Illinois Country. Macarty's actions give the impression that he had decided to build the fort near the old location from the start and neither hell, high water, nor the King of France could change his mind. To be four months away from your commanding officer is sometimes an advantage.

In August of 1753, Vaudreuil's successor, the new governor Kerlerac, wrote the Minister of the Marine that the Fort de Chartres project had been arranged prior to his appointment and that the cost was now estimated at 270,000 *livres*. By 1754, it was reported that the fort was largely completed, and although approval for construction had not yet been received from France, the work could not be stopped at this late date. By 1755 the construction had advanced to the point that contracts were made with Francois Hennet *dit* Sanschagrin to roof the fort's buildings and with Brunet and Couturier to dig a well. Some construction continued during the following year, but the garrison returned from Kaskaskia.

Figure 33: Interior of Fort de Chartres with ghosting of the Government House in right foreground.

The best description of the stone fort is from 1765 in the *Procès Verbal* upon the cession of the fort to the British by the vanquished French. This last fort was of stone, square with four bastions and contained about four acres within its walls. The *Procès Verbal* listed the buildings and gave the number of rooms, windows, doors and chimneys. All the buildings were of stone and had shingled roofs (Mr. Hennet's work). The storehouse and guard house were both about 90 by 25 feet in size; the Government house and the Intendant's house were approximately 86 by 32 feet; and the two barracks were 128 by 32 feet. In the bastions were the powder magazine, bake house, and prison. Two stone gates pierced the walls, one facing out toward the King's Road, the other toward the Mississippi. The main channel of the river ran about 500 feet from the south wall of the fort, providing easy access for the boats of the convoys.

This secure and well-built fort was surrendered to the British without a shot having been fired -- at Fort de Chartres, that is. The forces that led to its capitulation were at work far from the Illinois Country. The fate of Fort de Chartres must be understood in the context of the Illinois Country's status as a European colony.

FRENCH AND INDIAN WAR

> *During this conflict, French and Indian troops under the command of Coulon de Villier defeated British troops under the command of George Washington at Ft. Necessity on July 4, 1754.*

The Illinois Country was a small and not very important colony, when viewed in the grand scheme of European politics. Unlike the British colonists, who a few years later sought independence from the mother country, the Illinois French never considered separation from France. Their fate, therefore, was decided by events in the political arena.

France, Spain, and England long had been contending for power in Europe and for control of land and trade in the New World. Europe in the eighteenth century was almost continuously at war. One attempt to make peace was the Treaty of Aix-la-Chapelle in 1748, by which part of Acadia in Canada was ceded to England; however, the new boundaries between the English and French possessions were never defined.

The Ohio Valley was hotly contested: the English long had been pressing westward from the seacoast, vying with the French for control of this important waterway. With so few people in such a large area, European dominance basically rested on control of the trade with the Indians. Although in earlier years, French merchandise had been more highly prized by the Indians than the British, France's declining economic position caused their trade goods to become more expensive and less well-made than British goods. In fact, the French sometimes were forced to purchase British goods for use in their trade.

In the late 1740s, some of the Indian tribes friendly to the British began attacking Frenchmen, and tribes associated with the French were urged to join the British cause. Although the Illinois Indians remained faithful to the French, they occasionally wavered, for they were intermarried not only with the French, but also with the Miami and Piankashaw Indians, who were drawn toward the British side in the quarrel.

During the early 1750s, the French attempted to insure control of the Ohio by erecting a chain of forts from Lake Erie down the river. In 1754, a French detachment was sent to construct a fort at the forks of the Ohio, the present day site of Pittsburgh, Pennsylvania. Finding a small British force there engaged in the same occupation, the French drove them off and began building Fort Duquesne.

The escaping British soldiers carried the news of their defeat to George Washington, then a Colonel in the British Army, who was building a military road in the vicinity. Towards the end of May, Washington received word that a party of French soldiers was again in the vicinity. He and his men surprised and defeated the French force, killing among others, their commander, Sieur de Jumonville. Aware that the French

Figure 34: Canadian Militia (Frontier Service), 1750-1760

would retaliate, Washington returned to his base at Great Meadows, where a stockade with earthworks was constructed hurriedly and called Fort Necessity.

Soldiers, possibly including some from Fort de Chartres, were sent to avenge the French defeat, the group being commanded by Jumonville's brother, Coulon de Villers. The French attacked Fort Necessity on the morning of July 3rd, and the fighting continued throughout the day in a heavy rainstorm. In the evening, Villiers called for a parley. Recognizing the impossibility of defending the temporary fort against a long siege, Washington agreed to surrender. The British were allowed to keep their small arms and supplies. On July 4, 1754 Washington and his band of Virginians left unharmed.

The Seven Years War (1755-1763), called the French and Indian War in North America, decided the ultimate fate of the Illinois Country. Most Indian tribes supported the French and were important participants throughout the war. However, the French cause did not prosper; in 1758, one of France's most important posts, the Fortress of Louisbourg in Nova Scotia, fell and in 1760 Canada surrendered to the English forces.

France had never considered Louisiana to be as important a colony as Canada; indeed, Louisiana was a costly drain on the Royal Treasury -- about 800,000 francs a year. France's peace negotiator, the Duc de Choiseul, evidently felt Louisiana without Canada to be useless to France. Louisiana was used merely as a bargaining tool in the treaties with England and Spain. Under the Treaty of Paris, which ended the war, all Louisiana on the eastern side of the Mississippi River was given to England except for New Orleans, which became Spanish territory. Secretly, Louisiana west of the Mississippi was given to Spain.

In July of 1763, Governor D'Abbadie sent dispatches up river to inform Neyon de Villiers, commandant at Fort de Chartres, of the cession and to direct him to prepare for the arrival of the British. Although the French military officials accepted this reordering of their lives and property by the King, the Indians, who felt they had a prior claim to the land, did not.

Figure 35: Six pound cannon and carriage at Fort de Chartres.

Figure 36: Indian ally of the French, French and Indian War.

BRITISH AND AMERICANS

The British wished immediately to occupy the vital Mississippi Valley that they had acquired by treaty, but because of the danger of attacks by the Indians, this was delayed. The French had lived in peace with the Indians generally, but the Indians knew that in the British colonies the tribes were displaced and driven out as settlers moved in. So Pontiac, an Ottawa chief, was able to build an alliance from a number of tribes to oppose the British takeover.

The first British attempt to reach Fort de Chartres was made from Fort Pitt, going by boat down the Ohio River, but this had to be scuttled because of the Indians. Next, the British tried to come up the Mississippi; this, too, was foiled by the Indians. In June of 1764, Neyon de Villiers, the commandant, and all of the Fort de Chartres garrison, except for forty men, left for New Orleans, and St. Ange de Bellerive was placed in command. In 1765, two small British advance groups finally reached Fort de Chartres but shortly thereafter were forced to make a rapid withdrawal due to the hostility of the local Indians. Despite St. Ange's best endeavors, he was unable to

Private in little kilt

Grenadier

Sergeant and Officer. Battalion companies

Figure 37: British 42nd (Royal Highland) Regiment of foot, 1759-1760.

persuade the Illinois to accept the British. Tamarois, chief of the Kaskaskia, delivered the Illinois' decision to oppose the British.

Since you, with this English chief, asked me to make peace with his nation, my heart hesitated a long time on the decision it should make. I held several councils with my nation about the matter; and I did not find anyone who was of the opinion that peace should be accepted. All the red men possess scales in which are weighed our father the Frenchman and the Englishman. Whenever they raise it, the Englishman wins out and always weighs more. Why? Because he is filled with wickedness and he has not the white heart like our father [to the English officer]. Wherefore we ask you to leave here as quickly as you can, to rejoin your chief whom you can tell that the sentiment of the Illinois, like that of all their brothers, is to make war on you if you wish to come on our lands. Get out, move on as quickly as possible and tell your chief all you have heard, that we are the children of the French and that these lands are ours and no one claims them, not even other red men... Tell your chief to remain on his lands as we do all ours.

Ignoring this warning, a group of British soldiers again left Fort Pitt under Colonel Croghan. Intercepted near the mouth of the Wabash by hostile Kickapoo and Mascoutin Indians, they were taken prisoners to Vincennes. While they were there, most of the warring Indian nations finally came to sue for peace. Croghan did not continue to Fort de Chartres, but went to Detroit and sent instead Captain Stirling with the 42nd regiment out from Fort Pitt. Stirling arrived at Fort de Chartres on October 9, 1765 and the following day formally received the fort from St. Ange.

Stirling was under orders to administer an oath of allegiance to the citizens, but they asked for a delay in order to decide whether they were going to remain in their homes or to move across the river to the Spanish settlement. Some of the inhabitants were reassured by Gage's proclamation, allowing them to keep their religion.

... That his Majesty grants to the inhabitants of the Illinois the liberty of the Catholic religion as it has already been granted to his subjects in Canada ... That His Majesty, moreover, agrees that the French inhabitants, or others who had been subjects of the Christian King, may retire in full safety and freedom where ever they please, even to New Orleans, or any other part of Louisiana ... they may sell their estates ... transport their effects, as well as their persons without restraint...

Many preferred to move rather than to remain under the British. The village of Chartres was abandoned and the other settlements lost many inhabitants. Some sold all their goods; others took everything with them, including the door and window frames from their houses. They moved across the Mississippi to Ste. Genevieve and to the newly founded post of St. Louis.

According to the census reported by D'Abbadie to France in 1764, the population of Illinois was 1400. If this is correct, it represents a drop from 1752 and reflects the emigration of many of the inhabitants from the British side of the river to the Spanish side. The last commandant, St. Ange de Bellerive, left also for St. Louis with the remaining governmental officials, the judge and storekeeper, Lafebvre, and the clerk and notary, La Buxiere.

The departure of the French officials left the area without a civil government. Stirling appointed a judge and the militia captains were continued in their functions, but no other arrangements were made. This lack of a permanent civil government was the greatest weakness in the British administration of Illinois. Until 1774 when Louisiana was attached to Canada, Illinois was administered through the military organization from New York. Fort de Chartres was renamed Fort Cavendish. Although the new name was used for some official dispatches, it was largely ignored by the inhabitants.

Nature, too, was working its changes in the countryside. For many years, the Mississippi had been undercutting its bank near the village of Chartres and the fort. In the winter of 1771-72, it became obvious to the British that the spring floods would undermine the wall on the river side. The garrison was moved to Kaskaskia and the fort abandoned; the next spring, the wall on the river side and portions of two bastions were washed away. The British garrison remained in Kaskaskia until 1776 when they were recalled because of the American Revolution. Pierre de Rastel de Rocheblave was appointed British agent in Kaskaskia.

During the American Revolution, as in the French and Indian War, control of the inland waterways was an important strategic goal. From the Ohio River valley, the British could advance against the eastern colonies, forcing the Americans to fight on two fronts. Also, the British made treaties with the Indian tribes and encouraged them to attack American frontier settlements. The small size of the American population made defense of the outlying villages and fortifications difficult. In 1777, harassment of settlers in Virginia, Pennsylvania and Kentucky increased sharply as the British and their Indian allies attempted to draw off soldiers and supplies from the eastern seaboard.

A young Virginian, George Rogers Clark, who had been involved in the efforts to protect Kentucky, Virginia's new county, realized that the villages in the Illinois could be used by the British as a base for further raids into Kentucky. In 1778, Clark planned to take the offensive and to seize Kaskaskia and Vincennes from the British before such attacks could be launched. The new American government had made an alliance with France. He thought this would aid him in obtaining the allegiance of the French, who never had been happy under British rule. The purpose of Clark's campaign was publicly stated to be only the defense of Kentucky, but his private orders from Governor Patrick Henry were to capture the French villages.

With a hand-picked force of 175 men, Clark came down the Ohio River to Fort Massac, and then, with the assistance of captured American hunters, went overland to Kaskaskia. Surprising the British agent, Rocheblave, in his home, Clark and his men were able to take the town without opposition on July 4, 1778. Although not all the French wanted American rule, there was no active support for the British cause. The bell in the Kaskaskia church tower summoned the people, and their freedom from British rule was proclaimed. With its annexation to Virginia, the Illinois Country ceased to be a European colony, and became part of the new American nation.

Figure 38: George Rogers Clark addressing Native Americans at Cahokia

Figure 39: A soldier of George Rogers Clark's small army

TODAY: TOURING THE FRENCH COLONIAL AREA

Enjoy the story of colonial America in the heartland.

What is left of the French colony today? Of the seven French towns, Prairie du Rocher alone remains a small village. Ste. Genevieve has grown far beyond the bounds of the French village, but it is the only place where many eighteenth century structures have been preserved; here, one can sense what the old villages must have been like. Cahokia's past is represented by only a few buildings; urban sprawl has transformed its rural character. Kaskaskia was destroyed by floods in the 1880s. The Mississippi, which had flowed south of the peninsula on which Kaskaskia was situated, gradually began to break through the narrow strip of land between it and the Kaskaskia River. Eventually the Mississippi cut through and, being a larger and vastly more powerful stream, widened the Kaskaskia River bed, tumbling the village of Kaskaskia into the water. The village of Chartres, abandoned when the British arrived in 1765, also suffered greatly from erosion by the river, as did St. Philippe. The town plots were abandoned and forgotten. All that remains of eighteenth century St. Louis are place names and the street patterns.

Figure 40: Ste. Annes Militia re-enactors at Fort de Chartres.

A few French customs survive to this day; on New Year's Eve, La Guiannée singers in Prairie du Rocher make their rounds from house to house, singing their ancient song, *La Guiannée,* which was brought by the colonists from France. The singers today gather at a selected meeting place and go to homes where they have been invited. The first four lines of the song are sung outside the door of the house. The host then opens the door, inviting the group inside and the entire song is sung to the household and its guests.

> Bon soir le maître et la maîtresse et tout le monde du logis
> Pour le dernier jour de l'année la Guiannée
> vous nou devez.
> La Guiannée vous nous devez, dites-nous-le.
> Si vous voulez nous rien donner, dites-nous-le.
> On vous demande seulement un échinée.
> Une échinée n'est pas grand chose, ça n'a que de dix pieds de long.
> Et nous en ferons une fricassée de quatre-vingt-dix pieds de long.
> Si vous voulez nous rien donner, dites-nous-le.
> On vous demande seulement la fille aînée.
> Nous lui ferons faire bonne chère, nous lui ferons chauffer les pieds.
> Quand nous fûmes au milieu des bois, nous fûmes à l'ombre.
> J' ai attendu le coucou chanter et la colombe.
> Et le rossignol du vert bocage, l'ambassadeur des amoureux.
> Mai va-t-en dire à ma maîtresse qu'elle a toujours le cœur joyeux,
> Qu' elle a toujours le cœur joyeux, point de tristesse
> Toute les filles qui n'ont pas d'amant, comment vit-elle?
> Ce sont amours qui la réveillent et qui l'empêchent de dormir.

> [translation] Good evening master and mistress and all who live here.
> On the last day of the year la Guiannée is due us.
> La Guinannée is due us, tell us so.
> We ask only for a backbone of pork.
> A backbone is not a great matter, it is only ten feet long.
> We will make of it a fricassee ninety feet long.
> If you have nothing to give, tell us.
> We ask only for your eldest daughter.
> We will give her good cheer, we will warm her feet.
> When in the midst of the woods, we are in the shadows.
> We hear the cuckoo sing and the dove.
> The nightingale in the verdant grove, the ambassador of love.
> Go tell my mistress always to have a joyous heart,
> That she may always have a joyous heart, without sadness.
> All the girls who have no lover, how do they live?
> It is love which wakens her and which hinders her sleep.

Ste. Genevieve has a group, and Old Mines, Missouri, the location of Renault's mines, recently revived their Guiannée group.

In earlier days, La Guiannée singers would have collected food at each stop for their celebration and ball on Twelfth Night. This ball, on January 6th--Epiphany--the traditional end of the Christmas season, ceased to be held during World War II. It was

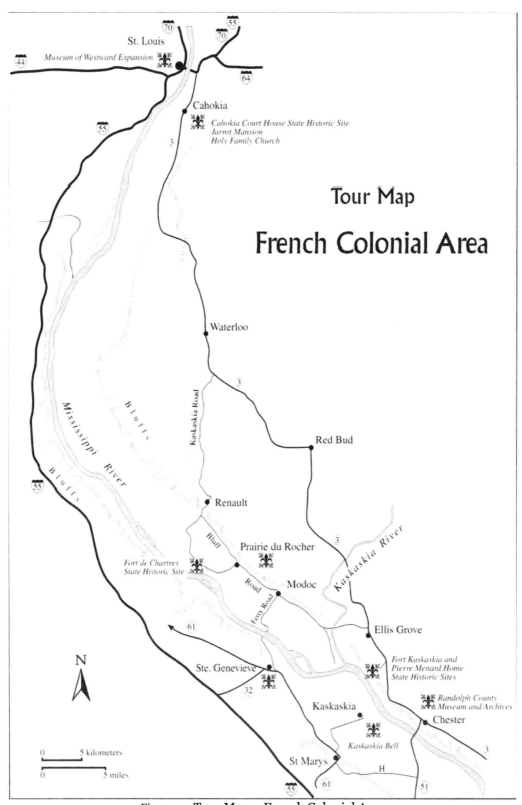

Figure 41: Tour Map – French Colonial Area

revived in Prairie du Rocher in 1976 and is now sponsored annually by La Guiannée Society on the Saturday closest to the 6th of January. At the Twelfth Night Ball, a king for the coming year is selected. A cake with four beans baked in it is cut and distributed to all the men present at the ball. The first to find a bean in his piece is the king, with the prerogative of choosing his queen. The finders of the other three beans become his court. The king and queen rule over all festivities for the remainder of the year. Cahokia holds a Fête du Bon Vieux Temps Ball the Saturday before Ash Wednesday sponsored by Fête Committee, Knights of Columbus #596, Illinois Historic Preservation Agency. The King's Ball, Fête du Bonne Temps La Guiannée, is held on the third weekend in January sponsored by the Cahokia Junior Women's Club. Ste. Genevieve's King's Ball Committee sponsors a Ball on the first Saturday in February at Ste. Genevieve.

Each year on the first weekend in June, the Illinois Historic Preservation Agency sponsors Rendezvous at Fort de Chartres. The two-day event recreates eighteenth-century activities including craft demonstrations of pottery making, basket weaving, wood turning, wine making and others. Contests are held in flintlock musket shooting. Period dancing, music, puppet shows, etc. are provided and recreated. Eighteenth-century military units march, attend to flag raising and lowering, and the firing of the cannon.

A driving or biking tour of the colonial area might begin at the town of Cahokia, Illinois. An information sign on U.S. Route 3/50 directs the visitor to Cahokia Courthouse, now a State Historic Site. Originally built in the mid-eighteenth century as a residence by Jean Baptiste Saucier, son of the designer of Fort de Chartres, the building served from 1793 to 1814 as a courthouse for St. Clair County. In 1904, the building, then abandoned and decaying, was dismantled and taken to St. Louis where it was reassembled for the Louisiana Purchase Exposition. After the Exposition, it was purchased by the Chicago Historical Society and a small structure constructed from its timbers in Jackson Park. The building stood there until 1938 when it was returned to Cahokia.

Standing now on its old foundation and incorporating some original timbers, the building is a good example of the Mississippi French architecture of post on sill construction. The posts originally had clay and rock fill between them (now cement). The roof is steeply sloped and there is a galerie [porch] around all four sides.

The Holy Family Church in Cahokia is on the opposite side of Routes 3/50. The old church of upright log construction was built in 1799 and was restored in the 1940s. Next door to the modern church is the Jarrot Mansion, owned by the Illinois Historic Preservation Agency. The brick home was built by Nicolas Jarrot who came to Cahokia from Maryland where he would have been familiar with the Federal style of architecture. The Jarrot house is called "Frontier Federal," a term coined for this building. Masonry work was begun in 1807, and the home probably was completed by 1808. Jarrot lived in the home until his death in 1820; his widow survived until 1875.

Figure 42: Jarrot Mansion, Cahokia, Illinois.

The Martin-Boismenue House, built ca. 1788, is in an area formerly known as Prairie du Pont (Prairie of the Bridge), but has been shortened by the Americans to "Dupo." A vertical log structure it was identified only when demolition had begun. Now it has been restored to its original appearance.

From Cahokia take Route 3 to I-255 to the Columbia exit, then continue on Highway 3. Three miles east of Waterloo (called Belle Fontaine by the French), is the Kaskaskia Road on your right. Winding through prairies dotted with limestone sinks (karst topography), the road partly follows the old Kaskaskia-to-Cahokia trail. At the "Y" in Renault (named for Philippe Renault, the Director of the Mines), the road angles to the right and continues down the bluff to the bottoms. From the stop sign at the bottom, you may take either the road to the left or the one straight ahead. The road on the left leads directly to Prairie du Rocher. This road along the bluff is a modern one, for the area was covered by vast shallow lakes and marshes in the eighteenth century. Today during wet springs, sheets of water often cover the old lake beds again.

The road that goes straight ahead leads to the little town of Kidd (Boxtown), and follows roughly the old road leading from St. Philippe. Turn left in Kidd; a ditched shallow swale on your right marks the old Coulée de Nau, an oxbow of the Mississippi which in French times formed the border of the Metchigamia Indian reserve. A mile or two beyond, just before the road bends sharply to the left, a ridge on the right was the location of a Metchigamia Indian village.

Fort de Chartres is next. The front walls of the fort have been reconstructed above the original French footings. The foundations of the barracks are marked by "ghostings," timbers outlining the shape and height of the original structure. Here, one can get a sense of what the fort really would have been like, and how impressive it would have been. In the eighteenth century, the stones, except for the cut stone around the gun and cannon ports, probably would have been covered with a smooth coat of mortar. This would prevent anyone from getting a foothold to climb the wall.

The original powder magazine is still standing, the oldest building in Illinois. It has been restored to its original appearance. The land gate, guard house and storehouse were reconstructed many years ago. The storehouse, now used as an office and museum, occupies the original foundation, but its doors and windows are not in the historic locations. The guard house was reconstructed in the 1940s in the early days of historic restoration. Present reconstruction of the Fort and upgrading of the structures is based on research, architectural, and archaeological studies.

Figure 43: Powder magazine at Fort de Chartres.

The river is no longer visible from the Fort. After damaging the walls in 1772, the Mississippi swung out again and presently is about a mile away from the Fort.

Rendezvous, a re-enactment of an eighteenth-century French traders' and trappers' fair is held annually on the first weekend of June. Special programs or activities are held at least once a month at the Fort.

On the left hand side of Highway 155 from the Fort to Prairie du Rocher, long strips of farmland stretch toward the bluffs. Often the original one or two arpent-wide land grants can be distinguished by ditches or by differences in crops. About a quarter of a mile from the Fort on the right was the location of the village of Chartres and the church of Ste. Anne. The village would have extended under the present levee towards the river.

The village hall in Prairie du Rocher was constructed in the old French style as a reminder of the town's heritage. Turn right on to the bluff road beyond it. On the main business street in town is a white building called the Creole House. Now owned by the Randolph County Historical Society, the house was built in the early nineteenth century but reflects the long tradition of French architecture in the area. The Creole House is open for special events or by arrangement.

Turn right on the street beyond the Creole House, go two blocks to Middle Street and turn left. A few blocks down is St. Joseph's Church. Originally, St. Joseph's was a mission from the Church of Ste. Anne at Fort de Chartres. The eighteenth century French parish registers and communion vessels from the church of Ste. Anne are preserved here. These items are not on display. Translations of the early church records are now available at the fort and on line. The present church was built in 1858.

Continue on Middle Street past the church, turn right and follow a small winding street. At the end of the block on the left is a white clapboard-covered house, the Melliere house, an excellent example of French construction techniques. On its western face, the outline of two enclosed galeries or porches can be seen. The house is privately owned and is not open to the public.

Follow the road across the railroad tracks. The cross road is Prairie du Rocher Street, part of the old King's Highway out to the Fort. Turn left and go out to the cemetery. A large aluminum cross marks the site of the original church of St. Joseph. Beside it a marker gives the history of the cemetery:

To mark the site of the sanctuary of the original church of St. Joseph and to commemorate the 250th anniversary of the first baptism recorded in the parish September 8, 1721. St. Joseph church and cemetery were located in the middle of the first village of Prairie du Rocher. Here lie buried the remains of Michigamea Indians, early French adventurers, black slaves, victims of wars, massacres, floods, and plagues. Veterans of all wars of the United States and pastors and parishioners of St. Joseph Church of three centuries – May they rest with God.

Two ancient gravestones lie within the bounds of the former sanctuary marking the graves of Father Gagnon and Father Luc Collet. Their bones were moved from the cemetery at the abandoned Ste. Anne's church to St. Joseph's in 1768. Only one gravestone in the cemetery has an inscription in French. Along the road near the front of the cemetery are many plain crosses of metal or wood, a French Canadian tradition.

Figures 44-45: Commemorative and original gravestones of Father J. Gagnon, 1743-1795.

From the front of the cemetery, the road formerly ran up to join the bluff road. The village of Prairie du Rocher used to surround the cemetery, but in the early nineteenth century, the settlement shifted closer to the bluffs to avoid flooding from the creek.

Return to the road by the church, drive to the bluff road and turn right; this is the old upper road. On the left side of the road after the first bridge is a sign marking the location of Modoc Rock Shelter. The rock shelter is a prehistoric Indian occupation dating from about 6000 B.C.

Just beyond the small community of Modoc, there is a choice of roads. The one straight ahead leads to the river ferry which crosses the Mississippi River to Ste. [28] Genevieve (which will discussed later). If you take the road to the left, a mile or so further along is a sign pointing to the lock and dam. The Kaskaskia Indian village was located about a mile down this road, but there is no surface indication of it today. The land is privately owned.

The bluff road ends at Highway 3. Turn right and follow the highway to the sign for Fort Kaskaskia and the Pierre Menard home. Fort Kaskaskia probably was built in the 1750s but may have replaced an earlier fortification. It was never a military fort but was used only for a retreat in times of danger. When the British came in 1765, the fort was in disrepair, and it was not restored. The British occupied a stockade structure within the town of Kaskaskia and named it Fort Gage. This name later erroneously has been applied by some to the fort on the bluff.

Figure 46: Pierre Menard Home.

Fort Kaskaskia is across the river from the former location of the village of Kaskaskia. The location can be seen from the edge of the bluff. Below the hill is the home of Pierre Menard, an Indian trader and the first lieutenant governor of Illinois. The home, constructed between 1799 and 1801, is in a combined French and American style. It has been beautifully restored and refurnished by the State of Illinois and is operated by the Illinois Historic Preservation Agency. Many programs and demonstrations are given on weekends at the Menard home.

Highway 3 goes on to Chester, where those interested in historical or genealogical research may consult several thousand documents from the French colonial period, some of which have been referenced here. Copies are located in the archives annex of the country courthouse. The records are calendared, indexed, and available for study during working hours. The originals are kept in a temperature and humidity-controlled vault in the office of the County Clerk.

Figure47: Randolph County Museum and Archives, Chester, Illinois.

Before Route 3 enters the downtown area of Chester, it crosses a road to the right leading to a bridge across the Mississippi. (The bridge can be reached also by going down the hill from the courthouse.) A few miles beyond the bridge in Missouri is Highway "H." Turn right and follow it to its end at Highway 61. Turn right to St. Mary. In St. Mary turn right on Highway "U" to cross the former channel of the Mississippi back into Illinois and onto Kaskaskia Island. This is the channel that the river occupied in the eighteenth and nineteenth centuries; it has filled in considerably since then. This piece of Illinois can only be reached through Missouri, to which it is now attached.

Follow the signs around the island to a small building maintained by the State of Illinois. Here is the bell from the old Kaskaskia church. The inscription on the bell reads, *"Pour l'église des Illinois par les soins du R.P. d'outeleau."* [For the church of the Illinois, a gift of Reverend Father D'outreleau]. Father D'outreleau was the superior of the Illinois missions.

The bell is called the Liberty Bell of the West, because it was rung on July 4, 1778 to signal Clark's arrival, and freedom from British rule. The bell is the property of the nearby Church of the Immaculate Conception, the direct descendant of the mission founded by Father Marquette in 1673. The bell was cast in La Rochelle, France in 1741 and has seen many changes over the years — the French colony, possession by the British, the arrival of the Virginians, incorporation into the United States -- and thus represents the heritage of the Illinois Country.

Go back to St. Mary and turn right on the highway. Follow this to Ste. Genevieve. Take the first road to the right, St. Mary's Road; along this road on the left you will see eighteenth-century French houses, some of which are open to the public.

On the right is *le Grand Champs* [the big field]; the village of Ste. Genevieve was located on the river side of this in the nineteenth century. In 1785, there was a major flood that inundated the homes there; after that, the inhabitants moved to higher ground.

Along the road is the Beauvais-Amoureux house. Built in the late eighteenth century, it is a fine example of *poteaux en terre* construction. The handhewn cedar logs are visible below the front porch and in the cellar. Another *poteaux en terre* house is the recently restored Bequette-Ribault house. Past the stop sign, the Green Tree Tavern is on the left; it has been restored to its original appearance.

On down the road and under the railroad bridge, the Bolduc house will be on the left. This was the first authentic French home in the Mississippi Valley to be restored to its original form.

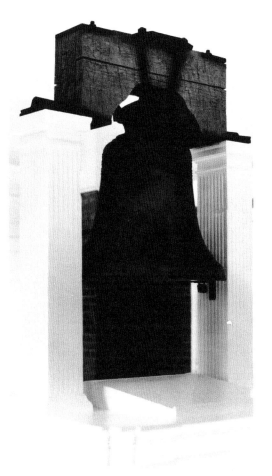

Figure 48: Liberty Bell of the West, Kaskaskia, Illinois.

Figure 49: Bequette-Ribault House, Ste. Genevieve, Missouri.

On other streets, there are many other buildings in town that are interesting for their architecture and history. The Felix Valle house, a 1-1/2 story ashlar stone structure has been restored by the Missouri Department of Natural Resources. The Guibord-Valle house, owned by the Foundation for Restoration, has the only remaining original casement windows and an excellent example of the typical roof trussing.

After the Bolduc house at the intersection of Main and Market on the right will be the Interpretive Center where information about the historic homes and tours can be obtained.

You can return to Illinois by the Ste. Genevieve/Modoc Ferry, which provides a good opportunity to view the mighty Mississippi.

Figure 50: Modoc Ferry crossing the Mississippi River, from Modoc, Illinois to Ste. Genevieve, Missouri.

If your trip takes you north to St. Louis, visit the Old Courthouse, the Museum of Westward Expansion, and the Gateway Arch. Collectively this complex is the Jefferson Memorial Expansion and is operated by the National Park Service. The French origins of St. Louis are interpreted at the courthouse, while the Museum of Westward Expansion tells the story of westward migration and growth after 1800. In addition, the Old Cathedral located within the complex represents the French Catholic roots of St. Louis and is the third church to serve the parish founded in 1770, the "Mother Church for St. Louis Catholicism."

We hope you have enjoyed your visit to the area of the 18th century French Illinois Country. Throughout the year there are activities planned that reflect this heritage. For more information on these, contact:
Cahokia Courthouse - cahokiacourt@sbcglobal.net
Fort de Chartres - www.fortdechartres.com
Ste. Genevieve - www.saintgenevievetourism.org

Figure51: The Old Cathedral, St. Louis, Missouri.

NOTES

Exploration and Early Settlement
Jolliet expedition: Thwaites vol. 59; Delanglez 1945.
Population of village: Thwaites vol. 60.
Story of Marie and Ako: Thwaites vol. 64.
Parish registers: Eschmann 1905.
Tamaroa mission: Palm 1931.

Founding of the French Communities
Description of Illinois: Page du Pratz 1774:58; Penicaut in French 1875
The Pélican: Rowland and Sanders 1932 III: 15; Higginbotham 1977: 138.
Chassin's letter: Rowland and Saunders 1932 II:279.
Penicaut's account: French 1875.
Arrival of Boisbriant: Archives Nationales des Colonies (ANC) B42:253-255.

Economy and Trade
Company of the Indies: Benians 1925
Return of colony to King: Louisiana Historical Society, Cabildo Archives Jan. 22-24. 173L
Amount of flour: Louisiana Historical Society Aug. 14, 1736.
Boat building contract: Dean and Brown 46: 11 :22: 1.
Pirogues: Anderson 1901: 145.
Notice for convoy: Dean and Brown 37:5:4:2.
Contract for voyage: Dean and Brown 31: 12:26:1.
Convoy leader: Pease and Jenison 1940: 159.
Missing brandy: Brown and Dean 1977:K544.
Convoy commander: Pease and Jenison 1940: 161.
Importance of post: Rowland and Sanders 1932 II:412.
Illinois voyageurs: Rowland and Sanders 1932 II:220.
Will of Franchomme: Brown and Dean 1977:K429.
Scarcity of coins: Surrey 1961: 103.
Payment in kind: Brown and Dean 1977: K36; K26; Kaskaskia Records 33:5:2: I.

Land and Village
Renault partnership: Giraud 1966 3: 179.
Seigneurial rights: Munro 1922.
Catherine's grant: Brown and Dean 1977:K4.
Organization of village: Alvord 1907.
Renault's house: Kaskaskia Land Records, Illinois State Archives, Book B:6.
House specifications: Dean and Brown 23.1 1.25.1.
Commandant's house: Brown 1977a.
Kaskaskia church: Dean and Brown 40:7: 17:2.
Ste. Anne's church: Dean and Brown 31.4. 15.3.

Population and Government
Census: Norton 1935 xxi-xxii; personal communication Kathrine Seineke
Garrison number: ANC 02 C50-5 I 1747; ANC CI3A: 35 1751
Post of the Illinois: Pease 1936:23.
Provincial council: ANC B43: 103- 107.
Chetivau desertion case: Brown and Dean 1977:K370.

Chetivau card cheating case: Brown and Dean 1977:K399.
Catin murder case: Dean and Brown 38: 12:20: 1.

Life in the Community
Becquet adoption: Dean and Brown 41: 1:5: 1.
Brunet donation: Dean and Brown 51: 11: 18:2.
La Plume donation: Dean and Brown 42:8:27: 1.
Olivier donation: Dean and Brown 49:4:21: 1.
Hullin's illegitimate child: Dean and Brown 26:5:23:1.
School master: Dean and Brown 60: 11:20: 1.
Medicines: Louisiana Historical Society: July I, 1739.
Food for hospital: Dean and Brown 40: 11:27: 1; 40: 11:27:2.
Code Noir: French 1851; Ekberg 2005.
Contract of Andre Duverger: Dean and Brown 25 :3: 12: 1 ; 43: 1 :28: 1.
Woman's dress: Brown and Dean 1977:K393.
Inventory: Dean and Brown 41:3:4:2.
Suit of clothes: Dean and Brown 40:5: 10: 1.
Legras' inventory: Brown and Dean 1977:K355.
de Tonty's inventory: Dean and Brown 37:6:23: 1.
Baron's inventory: Dean and Brown 48: 7 :6: 1.

The Military and the Fort
Assembly of the militia: Mereness 1916:76.
McCarty's order on the militia: Pease and Jenison 1940:305.
Organization of the military: Chartrand 1973 :62.
Soldier's life: Benson 1937:381.
Post of the Illinois: Rowland and Sanders 1932 III:514; ANC CI3 1326-374.
Building fort: Brown 1977a.
Description of second fort: Brown 1977a; Inventaire general bâtiments 14 Juin 1732 ANC C13B F581.
Design of fort: ANC C 13 38:20.
Location of fort: Brown 1977a; Pease and Jenison 1940:262;803; Tucker 1942 Plate XXIV.
Fort nearly completed: Pease and Jenison 1940:881.
Description of Fort: Alvord and Carter 1916:9 I.

French and Indian War
Ohio Valley competition: Pease and Jenison 1940:xxxvii.
Fort Necessity: Villers du Terrage 1904.
Progress of war: Pease 1936:xii.

British and Americans
Tamarois' speech: Alvord and Carter 1915:478.
Stirling's orders: Alvord and Carter 1916: 109.
Gage's proclamation: Alvord and Carter 1915:395.
D'Abbadie's census: Alvord and Carter 1915:209.
Stirling's appointments: Alvord and Carter 1916:xx.
Clark's campaign: Alvord and Carter 1915:478; Seineke 1981.

Today: Touring the French Colonial Area
La Guiannée: Brown 1977b.
Ste. Genevieve: Franzwa 1967.

BIBLIOGRAPHY

Alvord, Clarence W. *The County of Illinois*. Springfield: Illinois State Historical Library, reprinted from the Illinois Historical Collections, vol. 2, 1907

Alvord, Clarence W. and Clarence E. Carter (eds). *The Critical Period 1763-1765*. Springfield: Trustees of the Illinois State Historical Library, *Collections of the Illinois State Historical Library,* vol. 10, British series, vol. 1, 1915.

Alvord, Clarence W. and Clarence E. Carter (eds). *The New Régime 1765-1768*. Springfield: Illinois State Historical Library, *Collections of the Illinois State Historical Library*, vol. 11, British series vol. 2.

Archives Nationales de France, Archives Nationales des Colonies, Paris. Microfilm.
   (Many documents now available at the Archives nationales d'outre-mer and online.)

Balesi, Charles J. *The Time of the French in the Heart of North America*. Chicago: Alliance Française Chicago, with support of Mr. Barry MacLean, 1992.

Balvay, Arnaud. *L'Épée et la plume. Amérindiens et soldats des troupes de la marine en Louisiane et au Pays d'en Haut (1683-1763)*. Quebec: Presses de l'Université Laval, 2006.

Balvay, Arnaud. *Révolte des Natchez*. Paris: Félin, 2008.

Beers, Henry Putnam. *French and Spanish Records of Louisiana: A Bibliographical Guide to Archive and Manuscript Sources*. Baton Rouge: Louisiana State University Press, 1989.

Behrmann, Elmer H. *The Story of the Old Cathedral: Church of St. Louis IX. King of France*. St. Louis, MO: Church of St. Louis IX, 1949.

Belting, Natalia Marie. *Kaskaskia under the French Regime,* with a new foreword by Carl J. Ekberg. Shawnee classics. Carbondale: Southern Illinois University Press, 2003 [reprint from 1948 ed.].

Benians, E. A. "Financial Experiments and Colonial Development." *In Cambridge Modern History,* vol. VI: *The Eighteenth Century,* edited by A.W. Ward, G.W. Prothero, et al. New York: Macmillan Co., 1925.

Benson, Adolph B. (ed.) *Peter Kalm's Travels in North America: the America of 1750*, 2 vols. New York: Dover, 1966 [reprinted from 1937 ed.].

Brink, W.R. and Company. *An Illustrated Historical Atlas Map of Randolph County, Illinois*. [Philadelphia:] W.R. Brink and Co., 1875.

Brown, Margaret Kimball. "The Three Forts de Chartres." *Illinois Magazine* XVI (1977a):9.

Brown, Margaret Kimball. "La Guiannee." *Illinois Magazine* XVI (1977b): 10.

Brown, Margaret Kimball and Lawrie Cena Dean. *The Village of Chartres in Colonial Illinois 1720-1765*. New Orleans: Polyanthos Press, 1977.

Chartrand, René. "The Troops of French Louisiana, 1699-1769. Military Collector and Historian." *Journal of the Company of Military Historians*, XXV (1973):2.

Chartrand, René. *The Forts of New France: the Great Lakes, the Plains, and the Gulf Coast, 1600-1763*, illustrated by Brian Delf. Oxford/Long Island, NY: Osprey, 2010.

Dean, Lawrie Cena and Margaret Kimball Brown. *The Kaskaskia Manuscripts: 1714-1816: A Calendar of Civil Documents in Colonial Illinois*. Microfilm, n.d.

Delanglez, Jean. "Marquette's Autograph Map of the Mississippi River." *Mid-America: An Historical Quarterly*, vol. 27, no. 1 (1945): 30-53. http://archive.org/stream/midamericahistor27unse/midamericahistor27unse_djvu.txt

Eccles, W. J. *Government of New France*. Historical Booklet no. 18. Ottawa: Canadian Historical Association, 1968. http://www.collectionscanada.gc.ca/obj/008004/f2/H-18_en.pdf

Ekberg, Carl J. *French Roots in the Illinois Country: the Mississippi Frontier in Colonial Times*. Urbana: University of Illinois Press, 1998.

Ekberg, Carl J. *François Vallé and his World: Upper Louisiana before Lewis and Clark*. Columbia: University of Missouri Press, 2002.

Ekberg, Carl J., Grady Kilman, and B. Pierre Lebeau. *Code noir: the Colonial slave laws of French Mid-America*. Extended Publications Series no. 4. Naperville, IL: Center for French Colonial Studies, 2005.

Eschmann, C.J. "Kaskaskia Church Records." *Illinois State Historical Society, Transactions for 1904* (1905): 395-413.

Fadler, Theodore Jr. *Memoirs of a French Village: A Chronicle of Old Prairie du Rocher, 1722-1972*. [Prairie du Rocher]: Jiffy Printers, 1972.

Franzwa, Gregory. *The Story of Old Ste. Genevieve*. St. Louis: Patrice Press Inc., 1967.

French, B.F. *Historical Collections of Louisiana and Florida*. New York: Albert Mason, 1875.

Giraud, Marcel. *Histoire de la Louisiane française*, vol. 3: *L'époque de John Law (1717-1720)*. Paris: Presses universitaires de Frances, 1966.

Harrington, Jay. *New Light on Fort Necessity*. Richmond, Virginia: Eastern National Park and Monument Association, 1957.

Havard, Gilles. *Empire et métissages: Indiens et Français dans le Pays d'en haut, 1660-1715*. Sillery, Quebec: Septentrion / Paris: Presses de l'Université de Paris-Sorbonne, 2003.

Havard, Gilles and Cécile Vidal. *Histoire de l'Amérique française*, 3rd ed. Paris: Flammarion, 2008.

Higginbotham, Jay. *Old Mobile: Fort Louis de la Louisiana. 1702-1711*. Tuscaloosa: University of Alabama Press, 1991 [reprinted from 1977 ed.].

James, James Alton (ed.). *George Rogers Clark Papers 1771-1781*. Springfield: Trustees of the Illinois State Historical Library, *Collections of the Illinois State Historical Library*, vol. VIII, Virginia series vol. III, 1912.

Leavelle, Tracy Neal. *The Catholic Calumet: Colonial Conversions in French and Indian North America*. Philadelphia: University of Pennsylvania Press, 2012.

Louisiana Historical Society, Cabildo Archives, New Orleans.

Lowrie, Walter (ed.). *Documents, legislative and executive, of the Congress of the United States, in relation to the public lands*, 5 vols. Washington, D.C.: Duff Green, 1834. http://memory.loc.gov/ammem/amlaw/lwsp.html

Mereness, Newton D. *Travels in the American Colonies*. Cranbury, NJ: Scholar's Bookshelf, 2006 [reprinted from 1916 ed.].

Munro. W. B. *The Seigneurs of Old Canada. Chronicles of Canada*, vol. 5. Toronto: Brook & Co., 1922.

Norton, Margaret. *Illinois Census Returns, 1820*. Springfield: Trustees of the Illinois State Historical Library, *Collections of the Illinois State Historical Library*, vol. 24, 1935.

Page du Pratz, Antoine Simon. *The History of Louisiana*. London, T. Becket, 1774. Reprint New Orleans: J.S. Harmanson, 1947.

Palm, Sr. Mary Borgia. *Jesuit Missions of the Illinois Country 1673-1763*. Cleveland, 1931.

Pearson, Emmet F. "First Hospital in the Illinois Country." *Journal of the Illinois State Historical Society*. LXX:4, (1977): 299-301.

Pease, Theodore (ed.). *The French Foundations 1680-1693*. Springfield: Trustees of the Illinois State Historical Library, *Collections of the Illinois State Historical Library*. vol. 23, French series 1, 1934.

Pease, Theodore (ed.). *Anglo-French Boundary Disputes in the West 1749-1763*. Springfield: Trustees of the Illinois State Historical Library, *Collections of the Illinois State Historical Library*, vol. 27. French series 2, 1936.

Pease, Theodore C. and Ernestine Jenison (eds.). *Illinois on the Eve of the Seven Years War, 1747-1755*. Springfield: Trustees of the Illinois State Historical Library, *Collections of the Illinois State Historical Library*, vol. 29, 1940

Peyser, Joseph L. and José António Brandão (eds. and trans.). *Edge of Empire. Documents of Michilimackinac, 1671-1716*. East Lansing: Michigan State University Press / Mackinac Island State Park Commission, 2008.

Rowland, Dunbar and Albert Sanders (trans. and eds.). *Mississippi Provincial Archives 1701-1743. French Dominion*, 3 vols., Jackson: Mississippi University Press, 1927-1932, *vol. IV, 1729-1748* and *vol. V, 1749-1763*, rev. and ed. Patricia Galloway, Baton Rouge: Louisiana State University Press, 1984.

Seineke, Kathrine Wagner. *The George Rogers Clark Adventure in the Illinois*. New Orleans: Polyanthos Press, 1981.

Surrey, N.R.M. *The Commerce of Louisiana during the French Regime 1699-1763.* Studies in History, Economics and Public Law, vol. 71, no. 1. New York: Columbia University / Longmans, Green & Co., 1961.

Thwaites, Reuben Gold (ed.). *Original Journals of the Lewis and Clark Expedition, 1804-1806,* 8 vols. New York: Dodd, Mead and Company, 1904-1905.

Thwaites, Reuben Gold (ed.). *The Jesuit Relations and Allied Documents.* 73 vols. Cleveland: Burrows Bros. Co., 1896-1901.

Trudel, Marcel. *The Seigneurial Regime.* Historical Booklet no. 6. Ottawa: Canadian Historical Association, 1976. http://www.collectionscanada.gc.ca/obj/008004/f2/H-6_en.pdf

Tucker, Sara Jones. *Indian Villages of the Illinois Country.* Springfield: Illinois State Museum, 1975 (reprint from 1942 ed.).

Villiers du Terrage, Marc. *Les dernières années de la Louisianne Française.* Paris: E. Guilmote, 1904.